A DIY GUIDE TO STONE IN THE HOME

A DIY GUIDE TO STONE IN THE HOME

CHARLES MARGETTS

THE CROWOOD PRESS

First published in 2012 by
The Crowood Press Ltd
Ramsbury, Marlborough
Wiltshire SN8 2HR

www.crowood.com

British Library Cataloguing-in-Publication Data
A catalogue record for this book is available from the British Library.

ISBN 978 1 84797 399 3

Acknowledgements
I would like to thank the following people for their help in the preparation of this book. Firstly Martin and Barbara Moore for allowing me to use many photos which you can see in the following pages. Also to Andy Gough of Stonefix for the photos of ancillary products later in the book. Finally to David Stewart of Stoneclassics for help with the installation text and additional photographs.

Typeset by Jean Cussons Typesetting, Diss, Norfolk
Printed and bound in India by Replika Press Pvt Ltd

Contents

Introduction

Stone has been used in the UK home for thousands of years. The first part of this book will attempt to explain the different types of stone that are available and their advantages and disadvantages, and will then explain the array of different finishes. Next we will look at tile sizes and how you would choose the appropriate size and style to suit your property with real-life examples. Subjects covered will be the density of the various options as well as the merits of choosing locally sourced UK stone over material from Europe and further afield. Elements of architectural stone, such as stone fireplaces, are also covered, as well as more specialist areas such as choosing a stone worktop and specifying and choosing stone steps. Over recent years there has been a trend towards more sourcing of local stone, so we will examine this as well as how to choose a material that will complement a modern or contemporary property. The aim of this part of the book is to give the reader enough information to be able to identify the right product in the right size and style to suit their property.

Throughout history stone has been used for building. Some of the earliest surviving buildings from the ancient world were created from natural stone, such as the pyramids in Egypt, the statues on Easter Island and the stone circle at Stonehenge. The fact that these monuments survive thousands of years after their creation is testimony to the durability of natural stone and its ability to survive the ravages of the wind, weather and time. Ancient man recognized the durability and practicality of stone

This has continued over time. The Greeks erected the marble-clad Parthenon in Athens to pay homage to their gods. The Romans have left us the Circus Maximus, constructed from local travertine. In the UK, the builders of Westminster Abbey carved and worked Portland stone to create this towering structure, which still stands in central London. The Palace of Westminster and Big Ben, one of the UK's most iconic buildings, were carved from Cotswold Limestone

If you walk throughout the famous cities and civilizations of the world you will see their local stone used in their most famous buildings. It was only with the advent of more contemporary design that the use of stone was abandoned in favour of cheaper man-made substitutes. Stone became restricted to grand public buildings and the houses of the rich. The era of permanence and stability in design was over: the disposable society had arrived.

In recent years, however, the price of stone has come down. This has been driven by exploration and quarrying in new countries as well as advances in technology, which have led to vast cost savings in quarrying. What historically was not possible to quarry can now be done thanks to the forward march of technology.

The result of these changes has been the return of stone as a material for use within the home.

OPPOSITE: **Traditional Victorian decorative design for laying stone in a hallway. One corner has been clipped on every tile and a dark cabochon inserted. A border tile has also been cut from the main field stone on the floor.**
Martin Moore and Co.

Floors once covered with cheap carpet and life-expired vinyl are being replaced by limestone, travertine or marble. Laminate and ceramic worktops are being replaced by granite slabs. Bland shower designs and mundane vanity tops are being replaced by antiqued marble mosaic and warm travertine tiles.

If you are planning a building refurbishment or extension it is likely that you will consider the use of stone somewhere within the project. Much of what you may have heard regarding stone will be the normal mix of fiction and truth. The overall aim of this book is to guide you through the selection process to ensure you select the right stone for your project, and to ensure the installation is carried out correctly. The end result should be that you have a hard-wearing and durable floor (or worktop, or fireplace) that will a feature of your home for many years to come.

PART I

Selecting Your Stone

The first section of this book will deal with the process of selecting the right material for your project. It will describe all of the different types of natural stone and their characteristics. It will discuss the array of different stone sizes and finishes available and will give real-life examples as to how to obtain the best look for a space. This section then goes on to consider how stone can be used to best advantage in the main rooms of the home, not just for flooring, but also for other architectural details, such as fireplaces, steps, staircases and countertops. The final part will analyse the different places you can purchase stone and their respective advantages and disadvantages.

The aim of this section is not to suggest that any particular approach is best but to provide the reader with all the necessary information so that they can make an informed decision about which stone to buy, in what size and in what finish.

CHAPTER 1

Types of Natural Stone

There are many types of natural stone that can be used in the home. This chapter attempts to define the differences between the types, together with each stone's strengths and weaknesses, so that the reader can make an informed choice on the right one for their project.

LIMESTONE

Limestone is the most common material used for flooring from the natural stone range. It tends to give a matt appearance with scattered fossils or veins across the surface, which tends to complement the British home. It is also possible to use stone that has traditionally been quarried in the UK such as Lincoln, Portland, Cotswold and Bath stone – all materials many people have seen before. There are also lesser-known English limestones, such as the range of Purbeck limestones or the material that is still quarried in the Forest of Dean. Over recent years, with the trend to use more heritage materials as well as concerns over minimizing the miles to market a product travels, there has been a resurgence in the UK stone industry and there is now a greater variety of materials and finishes on offer than there has been for many years. Due to the scale of production in most English quarries, however, stone from England does tend to cost more than material from overseas.

There is a vast range of other materials available from Western Europe and further afield. French stone has traditionally been used in this country. Many French stones are sourced from Burgundy, where stone production is the second biggest employer after the production of wine. There was the recent incident of Caen limestone being used in the redevelopment of the British Museum

A traditional Cotswold limestone floor. The tiles have been aged by pillowing the edges and then chiselling the sides to give this classic traditional look. Martin Moore and Co.

A common use of stone is for decorative features around the home. Stone has traditionally been used for fireplaces for hundreds of years and can provide an effective centrepiece to any room.
Martin Moore and Co.

instead of Portland. Anyone who has travelled through Belgium cannot have failed to notice the Belgian blue limestone, which is used for everything from kitchen worktops to pavements and kerbstones. Over recent years, with increasing industrialization of the developing world, limestone is also now supplied from far-flung countries such as Israel, Egypt, Tunisia and Vietnam as the existence of global shipping networks make it inexpensive to offer on the UK market. The scale of production in these countries, combined with

low labour costs, often means that though these materials have travelled much further to market, they are less expensive to purchase than English or Western European equivalents.

Most limestone was formed during the Jurassic period by deposits of shells collecting on the sea bed. Over time more and more material collected and the lower levels became more and more compressed. The colour of the stone depends on the minerals prevalent in each area. Eventually the prehistoric seas dried up and became land,

A clean, contemporary modern limestone in a honed finish. Martin Moore and Co.

leaving a resource that modern-day man has not been slow to exploit.

Limestone is a sedimentary rock found in abundance around the world, which has been used in construction for millennia. It is often used for many other internal uses apart from flooring, for example as fireplaces.

There are many different types of limestone, varying in colour, strength and porosity, among other things. It is important when selecting a limestone for a floor to choose a medium- to high-density stone. This will be more durable and much easier to seal and to maintain. Most retailers will be able to tell you the density figure for each product; if in doubt, ask the retailer for a sample. It is easy to look at the sides of a sample (which will not have been worked) and examine the number of air holes. This will give you an idea of the density. You can also gain an idea from comparing the weight of tile samples. A heavier tile is heavier because it is denser and therefore is a more practical choice for flooring. Softer stones are much more suitable for carving and tend to be used for fireplaces and architectural details, such as cornices and windowsills.

For a limestone to be suitable for extraction for building use it must be both possible and cost-effective to quarry large blocks from the seam. Once the block is cut it is them sliced into slabs. Some of these slabs are used for the manufacture of worktops. Others are put through a tile line to be cut into tiles. If the seam is the right size it should provide a continuous supply, but it should be noted that stone is a natural material and it is perfectly possible for the same limestone to vary in colour and shell content over time. It is therefore vitally important to gain a full understanding of a material by going to look at a large display floor. Any competent retailer will be happy to show you a large area of stone and explain the variation you will get.

It is also important to understand the characteristics of any natural stone. Limestone varies greatly in density from very soft materials that are only suitable for carving for fireplaces and similar architectural stone right through to material that virtually has the density of granite.

Limestone is the most commonly used stone for interior design in the UK because it has soft matt tones and can suit any scheme from modern to traditional.

As all limestones are porous to a greater or less degree it is essential to seal it, whatever the use you are planning for it. There are numerous types of sealant available. The best type is a non-filming silicone impregnating sealant, which enters the stone and protects it against dirt and water. The sealer sits in the tiny pores on the surface of the stone and not actually on top of the stone, and so cannot be worn away by heavy foot traffic. It is important to use the brand of sealer recommended by the retailer. Sealing must be carried our properly on installation. As long as this is done then resealing can be carried out every four to five years.

If you intend to use limestone outdoors it is necessary to determine the degree of frost-resistance of the stone to be used. Some limestones are completely frost resistant and will provide a practical, durable surface outside. The top surface on a non-frost resistant stone, however, will suffer from frost heave. This is caused by water entering the tiny pores in the top of the stone. When the water freezes it expands and the surface of the stone begins to weaken and will eventually flake away. This is very unsightly and clearly should be avoided. It is always essential to provide an adequate fall to ensure proper drainage and avoid pooling of water on the surface.

SLATE

Most people have a strong impression of what slate looks like from its use for flooring and roofing tiles across the UK. It is quarried by lifting out large slabs from the rock face and then splitting them into two pieces. Slate is available in both tile and flagstone format. A material is usually classified as slate if it splits along natural plane of weakness to form either tiles or flagstones. Thus the riven surface is natural and not formed by any machine process, and is consequently an extremely durable material, resistant to frost and capable of being used both indoors and out.

Slate was traditionally quarried in the UK in Wales, the Lake District and Caithness in Scotland. These heritage suppliers are still producing good quantities of material and over recent years

A traditional Lake District slate. It has been used in tile format on the floors and walls, and as a countertop.

have seen a growing demand for their product from overseas. Most people think of slate as being black but there is a variety of unusual colours, which come from Welsh slate and Lake District material in particular.

The continual push to source lower cost materials has led to a lot of slate being imported from Brazil, Spain and Portugal. This slate is more competitive in price but does not have the same range of colours. However, it tends to be available in larger sizes, which is important if you are intending to lay a flagstone floor. A variety of treatments have been identified to antique slate, including washing the surface with acid. Slate is also porous and needs to be sealed on application and then resealed every four to five years.

Slate is essentially hand-split or riven, resulting in a rustic surface, whilst the edges are more uniform, being diamond sawn. It is an ideal material to choose if you are looking for a dark, inexpensive, rustic material. However, you should be aware that dark floor colours tend to absorb a lot of natural light and it is a good idea to take home a couple of sample tiles to understand how it will look on your project.

MARBLE

Marble is a material that has been used for internal flooring since Roman times but has gone in and out of fashion many times. This tends to be based on whether the strong colours and markings within the stone suit the interiors of the day. At the time of writing, after a long period where it was rarely used, marble is starting to be chosen more frequently in the UK again. It has always been the most popular stone in some areas of the world (such as the Middle East and across the Mediterranean) as the colours tend to suit the interiors in these areas.

Marble is geologically similar to limestone, being formed at a similar time, by metamorphism of sedimentary carbonate rocks. The main difference is that marble beds have generally recrystallized over time, and this can be seen from the prominent veins and quartz in the surface. It gains its primary colour from the key minerals in the area where it is sourced: white marbles contain higher amounts of dolomite; green marbles contain high amounts of serpentine, resulting from originally high levels of magnesium limestone or dolostone with silica impurities; and red and brown colours are signs of high levels of iron oxide in the stone. These various impurities have been mobilized and recrystallized by the intense pressure and heat of the metamorphism.

Historically, marble is most common as a flooring material in the Mediterranean area, where it was – and still is today – extensively quarried. Colours vary from white, beige and all the way through to rich greens and greys. Over recent years it has tended to be used for flooring in more contemporary bathroom schemes as it is more colourful and visually stronger than most limestones. It is porous by nature and it is essential that it is sealed upon installation and resealed every four to five years to maintain the surface.

There are many different grades of the more popular marbles. It is always wise to pay a little more and source premium-grade marbles. These will be more consistent and have less colour and vein variation than their commercial equivalents. Do not source a marble simply by looking at a small sample. It is very important to understand the range of colour and vein variation in the stone. Any competent retailer dealing with marble will be able to show you big enough display for you to understand the stone.

The most notable English marble is Purbeck marble, which is sourced from the Isle of Purbeck in Dorset. This has been quarried since Roman times and is still extracted in small quantities today. It can be seen in Westminster Abbey and the Tower of London, as well as other historic buildings across the UK.

GRANITE

Granite is an igneous rock composed of quartz, feldspar and mica. It is molten rock that has solidified under pressure. It is mainly sourced from India and Brazil, but other well-known granites are also found in Angola and Finland. Depending on the mineral content, it will range in colour from black to brown, pink, green or off-white. A very hard material, it is excellent for worktops but tends to be less common for flooring due to its dark tones and shiny surfaces. If you are considering

purchasing granite it is worth visiting a large granite importer so that you can see large pieces of granite and gain a full understanding of the stone. Granite is also porous (although less so than any other natural stone) and therefore needs to be sealed correctly on installation and resealed every four to five years after that.

TERRACOTTA

Terracotta is simply fired and baked clay. It is the warmest natural floor you can find and will add a cosy feel to any property. Terracotta ranges from soft pink tones right through to rich red colours. The colour is simply based on the colour of the clay in the area from which it is sourced. Thus the terracotta tiles both belong to and are derived from their surroundings; they are indigenous to it.

The clay is moulded into shapes and then fired in a kiln to harden it. It was historically most common along the southern coasts of Europe and was used as a floor tile and a roof tile. It was also used as an architectural material in the Arts and Crafts Movement. The Natural History Museum

TOP: **A clean, contemporary calico polished marble used in a bathroom.**

BOTTOM: **An aged marble floor. You can clearly see the large quartz veins in some of the tiles. Marble can be a more striking floor than a traditional limestone.**

This French antique Blanc Rose floor clearly shows the warm pink and red tones that can be obtained in a terracotta floor. This is the warmest natural material you can install as a floor.
Martin Moore and Co.

has an ornate terracotta glazing on the front of the building. Once laid and waxed, the tiles' colour and texture offer a calm, natural background for any room within any property – old or new.

By its nature, terracotta produces a more rustic farmhouse look. It is generally found in smaller sizes and is thicker than most limestones or marbles, but has a warm, cosy hue that these other stones cannot offer. Terracotta is porous and therefore it needs to be sealed correctly on installation. There are a variety of other finishing techniques that have been used to strengthen the natural warmth of this material. The most common of these is to wax the terracotta after sealing with either beeswax or an equivalent modern product. The wax enhances the natural warmth of the clay. It needs to be resealed and rewaxed every four to five years.

A piece of unfilled travertine prior to installation. You can clearly see the holes in the surface, which must be filled with grout during installation.

The colours of terracotta are associated with the Mediterranean and at the time of writing it is most commonly sourced from Spain and Portugal. It is another material that has gone in and out of fashion based on the interior trends of the time, but is currently coming back into fashion. Again, it is essential not to base your choice on a small sample but to see a larger display floor to understand the variations in colour and tone. It is possible to source antique reclaimed terracotta to provide a very traditional floor. This is common in France, where there is a growing market and steady supply.

TRAVERTINE

Travertine is a natural stone that has become increasingly prevalent in the UK over the last twenty years due to its soft colours and competitive prices. It remains, at the time of writing, the most cost-effective form of natural stone flooring.

Travertine is similar to limestone in geological formation and was formed at around the same time. The distinctive feature of travertine is that it will have a certain amount of holes in it, caused by the fact that travertine was often found in areas where there had been hot mineral spring. The holes in the travertine were formed where the water used to bubble through the ground. It tends to have soft swirly patterns to the stone and is found in colours from soft creams right through to walnut.

Travertine is commonly found in big blocks and is frequently used in Italy and elsewhere as a building material. There are several different grades used for flooring. Premium travertine has fewer holes and therefore is a more dense, less varied and more durable floor than commercial-grade travertine.

There are two ways of dealing with the holes in the travertine. You can fill them with resin in the quarry. This gives a smooth ivory finish to the tile. The filler will not suffer from discolouration but over time it is possible that small chunks of filler could come loose. There is no solution to this apart from refilling the stone. The other way of dealing with the holes is supplying the floor tile to site unfilled and filling the holes with grout on site.

The same tile when it has been installed. If you look closely you can see where the tiler has skimmed the floor with grout and filled in the holes.

This tends to give a darker finish and over time the grout will discolour and blend into the stone. From my experience, if you are after a contemporary, clean look it is far better to use resin-filled travertine. If you wish for a more antique look, the grout-filled travertine is perfectly acceptable. The latter also tends to be less expensive as less work has been carried out on it (because it has not been filled).

Travertine was originally sourced from Italy, but over recent years the demand for cheaper materials means that most travertine now comes from Turkey or Iran. If you intend to choose a travertine it is wise to check carefully on the density and durability of the stone.

It has become very popular in the British home due to its light, warm colours and the fact that it tends to be the least expensive of any natural stone tile. As with all natural stone, however, travertine is porous and it must be sealed properly on installation and resealed every four to five years. Travertine is particularly popular for bathrooms owing to the warm tones, as well as the fact that it is easy to obtain precut worktops, dado rails and mosaics inexpensively.

SANDSTONE

Sandstone is a sedimentary rock that consists mainly of sand-sized minerals or rock grains, and also commonly contains quartz and/or feldspar. It goes without saying that it tends to reflect the colour of the sand from the region it is sourced from. Therefore, you tend to notice the red sandstone in many buildings in Cheshire, the beige sandstone found near to Horsham in Sussex and other local examples.

The formation of sandstone involves two key stages. First, a layer or layers of sand accumulates as the result of sedimentation, either from water (as in a stream, lake, or sea) or from air (as in a desert). Typically, sedimentation occurs by the sand settling out from suspension; that is, it stops being rolled or bounced along the bottom of a body of water or ground surface (for example, in a desert). Finally, once it has accumulated, the sand is compacted by the pressure of overlying deposits and cemented by the precipitation of minerals within the pore spaces between sand grains to become sandstone.

There are two major types of sandstone found in the UK. The first type is commonly known as

Yorkstone, and is quarried across Derbyshire and Yorkshire. The colour varies from green/grey right through to blue tones, depending on the location of the quarry. It is a dense, durable, coarse material, which is commonly used for external terracing or paving due to the fact it is frost-resistant. However, because most quarries are small and the level of production is not high, the cost per metre for extraction tends to be higher than non-UK alternatives and therefore the price to market is also higher.

The other major range of sandstone available is imported from India. There is a large range of colours to this material ranging from buff to grey tones. They tend to have a split face and a riven surface, which makes them perfectly suitable for external use. The vast majority of these materials are also frost-resistant. They are quarried on a vast scale, which brings the price down, making them the most economical way of doing external terracing in natural stone. Indian sandstone is generally as cheap as most aggregate alternatives. The soft, natural, matt colours of Indian sandstone tend to complement most UK housing stock, which has led to widespread use across the country.

All sandstone is porous and therefore it is essential that any sandstone floor is properly sealed upon installation and then resealed every four to five years.

Due to the way it is quarried most sandstone is currently either 25mm thick or of varied depth. This can in some cases create issues with floor heights, making sandstone a difficult option to pursue for such projects.

OTHER MATERIALS

There are other natural stones that can be used for internal flooring, such as basalt or quartzite, both available in the UK. It is important to explore the properties and variation of any other natural product with a potential retailer to ensure they are suitable for your project. Attributes to consider are durability, porosity, density and colour variation. As these stones are less common they tend to be more expensive. It is worth reiterating at this point that all natural stones are porous and will need sealing correctly on installation as well as resealing periodically over time.

REPLICA MAN-MADE FLAGSTONES

There are a small amount of replica man-made flagstones available in the UK. They tend to have a concrete base with a layer of crushed stone aggregate on top, which is formed into a mould. The price is similar to aged limestone floors, but man-made stones are more consistent in colour. The layer of aggregate tends to be quite thin, however, and it is possible that if used in a busy area, the aggregate can be worn away, leaving the concrete base exposed. Man-made stones also need to be sealed like any other natural stone.

STONE VERSUS PORCELAIN OR CERAMICS

Retailers who market stone or porcelain have often tried to exaggerate the advantages of each to the detriment of the other (which is most cases they do not sell). I would maintain that neither is the perfect bullet-proof, maintenance-free floor and have outlined the key characteristics of each below.

Stone
- Stone is a better conductor of heat than porcelain and therefore is more suited to underfloor heating.
- When you seal a stone floor you also seal the grout, which gives it protection from dirt and means it will discolour much more slowly than a porcelain floor.
- There is a wide range of aged and antique stone floors. At the time of writing you cannot age or antique porcelain or ceramics effectively.
- It is difficult for a man-made product, such as a porcelain or ceramic, to replicate the natural characteristics of a stone floor.

Ceramics/Porcelain
- Ceramics and porcelain do not need to be sealed and are therefore easier to maintain than stone, as well as cheaper to install.
- There are now ceramics and porcelains that are very close copies of honed stone and are suitable for contemporary projects.

A traditional Bath stone laid in an aged and pillowed format to complement this traditional property. Martin Moore and Co.

- Large tiles tend to be more cost-effective as a porcelain or ceramic rather than a stone floor.

Clearly neither material is necessarily better than the other. The key decision for a potential user is to decide which material with its individual characteristics is the most suitable for their project in terms of the look and the practical characteristics

STRENGTHS AND WEAKNESSES OF EACH STONE

This section gives a summary of the strengths and weaknesses of different types of stone.

Limestone

Advantages
- The matt tone and soft colours tend to suit most UK houses.
- A vast variety of colours and textures gives the client a good chance of finding something to complement their scheme, whichever part of the house is being redeveloped.
- Limestone is easy to antique/age successfully and there is a wide choice of different finishes.
- The wide range of prices suits all needs.
- Worktops/large pieces/steps are easy to obtain with some materials.
- Limestone is a conductor and is therefore particularly suited to underfloor heating.

Disadvantages
- The vast array of different stones makes it difficult for a client to be certain they are buying the correct product for their purposes.
- Limestone needs to be sealed properly upon installation.
- Only a limited range of stones are frost-resistant and thus suitable for external use.

Slate

Advantages
- Slate is a durable, hard material that can often be used outside.
- It gives a natural, rustic feel where required.
- Slate can be cost-effective to obtain in larger sizes.

- The material is practical and easy to look after.
- It can be an effective alternative to granite as a worktop.

Disadvantages
- Slate only comes in a narrow range of colours, which are predominantly dark, so it can be more difficult to find stones to complement some interior schemes.
- Slate can be prone to scratching, wherever it is used.
- It needs to be sealed properly upon installation.

Marble

Advantages
- It is easy to create a contemporary, modern look with marble.
- Marble tiles come in a wide variety of colours and sizes.
- Marble is a conductor of heat and is therefore particularly suited to underfloor heating.
- It can be particularly effective in a bathroom, where stronger colours are required.
- It is easy to obtain worktops/large pieces where required.
- The veining and marking prevalent in many marbles can make it particularly effective as a design feature.

Disadvantages
- Strong colours and markings make marble unsuitable for some schemes.
- The variety of antiqued or aged materials available is limited.
- It is essential to see a large display floor to understand the variation in any marble.
- Marble is porous and needs to be sealed properly on installation.
- Only a limited range of materials are frost-resistant if you are aiming for matching stone indoors and outdoors.

Granite

Advantages
- Granite is the hardest and most durable of natural materials.

- It is very easy to maintain and look after.
- The stone contains striking colours and markings.
- This is the most practical natural stone to use as a worktop. It is virtually impervious and is resistant to acid.

Disadvantages
- Granite tends to have very strong colours that make it difficult to use for a scheme as a floor tile.
- Only a narrow range of floor tiles is available.
- It tends to be slightly thicker than other stones in tile format.

Terracotta

Advantages
- The warm, rustic tone from terracotta tiles cannot be replicated in any other natural stone.
- Small tile sizes and antique patina go well in any rustic scheme.
- Terracotta is a very effective conductor of underfloor heat.
- A terracotta floor is the perfect complement to a farmhouse kitchen.

Disadvantages
- Terracotta tends to be thicker than limestone, marble, granite and travertine because it is made from fired clay.
- The colour range available is narrow and commonly varies from salmon pink to red.
- It is impossible to get tiles larger than 30cm × 30cm due to the way terracotta is produced.
- Terracotta is porous and needs to be sealed properly on installation.
- Terracotta is not frost-resistant and therefore cannot be used externally in the UK.

Travertine

Advantages
- Travertine has light colours with patterns, which is particularly attractive.
- It is the most cost-effective of natural stones.
- Travertine can easily be aged or antiqued to provide a more traditional look.

- Travertine can be obtained in large tile sizes and worktops at competitive prices.
- A wide variety of tile sizes and dado sizes are produced as standard, giving plenty of options for tile sizes.

Disadvantages
- Unfilled travertine needs to be filled on site. This is normally done with grout, which can discolour over time.
- Filled travertine will be subject to small holes developing as the filler pops out over time.
- The range of colours is quite narrow.
- Travertine is porous and needs to be sealed properly on site after installation.
- There is a limited range of frost-resistant materials that can be used outside in the UK.

Sandstone

Advantages
- Most stones are frost-resistant and can be used externally.
- It is a very cost-effective stone.
- The split-face, riven surface makes a perfect textured, non-slip surface.
- Sandstone used externally often suits the look of UK properties.

Disadvantages
- Sandstone tends to be supplied in thicker depths, making it unsuitable for some projects, especially for internal use.
- It is not available in a honed finish, again making it difficult to use internally.
- Sandstone cannot easily be aged or antiqued and therefore the range of finishes is very limited.
- Sandstone is porous and therefore needs to be sealed properly on site after installation.

Replica Man-Made Flagstones

Advantages
- Man-made stones tend to be consistent in colour.
- Replica flagstones tend to be fairly cost-effective.
- Can be used internally or externally, giving a harmonious indoor/outdoor look.

The front face of two pieces of travertine. The square piece is commercial-grade travertine and has many more holes in it than premium-grade stone; the white patches are filler in the holes. The rectangular piece is a premium-grade piece of stone and will be much more durable as it has less filler.

The same two pieces of stone as the photograph above, but showing the rear face. From the back you can clearly see the large number of holes in the square tile in comparison to the rectangular tile. The back of a piece of stone always gives more clues than the front as to the quality of the tile.

Disadvantages

- Man-made stones are no longer less expensive than natural stone.
- They are not suitable for heavy use areas.
- They tend to have a slightly artificial sheen.
- They still need to be sealed just the same as natural stone.
- The range of sizes and finishes is limited.

COSTS

Stone has long been associated with wealth and prestige and until recently was primarily used for high-end residential and commercial projects. With advances in quarrying, technology and the opening up of new marketplaces, however, stone has become affordable to many domestic households whether as flooring, a fireplace, kitchen counter top or a bathroom vanity top.

Whether you are looking for flooring for a new home or simply upgrading one room in the house the table below will give you an idea of the various costs involved with the various different types of stone.

There are many factors that can effect cost, which does not necessarily have anything to do with the quality of the stone. The price is determined by the cost of getting the material out of the ground and then getting the product to market. UK-based quarries, which are generally small scale, are often not very competitive.

It is always important to ensure you are purchasing premium-grade stone, as this will contain fewer imperfections, such as veins and colour variation.

Any stone subject to any form of antiquing or ageing will be more expensive to purchase than in its honed format because the antiquing is a separate process carried out on the stone after cutting and therefore incurring a higher manufacturing cost. It also follows that hand-finished antiquing processes are more expensive than machine-based antiquing (such as a tumbled finish) and therefore the retail price tends to be higher. It is obviously up to the client to decide whether the hand-finished treatment is superior in appearance to the less expensive machine-antiqued finish.

Slab costs tend to reflect primarily the ease of sourcing big pieces of the stone and do not necessarily have any correlation with the cost of the tile. It is perfectly possible to find a less expensive tile that is more expensive in slab form. The other major element of cost in terms of making counter tops, bath tops, sink tops and so on from slab is the amount of labour it takes to fabricate and install the finished piece. The more cutouts, drainer grooves and the more ornate edge detail is applied, the greater is the time required to finish the piece and the higher is the cost. The thickness of the slab can also cause the cost to fluctuate. The table below is intended as a guide; it is very wise to do research and to obtain prices from several retailers to ensure you are getting a fair price:

Stone	Tile	Slab
Limestone	££–££££	££–£££
Travertine	£	££
Marble	£££	£££
Slate	£ to £££	£££
Machine-aged stone	£££	n/a
Hand-aged stone	££££	n/a
Antique reclaimed stone	£££££	n/a
Ceramic/porcelain	£–£££	n/a
Corian/quartz	n/a	££££
Granite	££££	££–££££
Terracotta	££	n/a
Man-made replicas	£££	n/a

The cost of all these items is governed by world affairs. At the time of writing the pound is relatively weak against the euro. The fall in value of the pound has made products purchased in euros much more expensive to import and less competitive, so materials purchased in dollars from countries such as Egypt, Turkey and India are the most competitively priced on the UK market at the time of writing. As these are primarily limestone and travertine these are the most competitive products. However, this situation could easily change as time moves on, and it is worth considering this when making your choice.

FINISHES

Over recent years stone suppliers have continually sought to develop their stones by offering them in a variety of different finishes. Below is a list of the key terms to enable the reader to select the appropriate finish. It is quite possible for many stones to be available in all or most of these finishes. The aim of this section is to give the reader the knowledge, once they have identified the type of stone they want, to make an informed choice on the ideal finish.

Contemporary Finishes

Honed

A honed tile is a tile with a flat, even top and straight sides with no edge detail. It is customary, though not obligatory, to use honed tiles in more contemporary schemes for kitchens and hallways and use an aged stone in a more traditional scheme. However, honed tiles are more commonly used for bathrooms as they can be used on the floors and walls.

A honed tile is created in the quarry by cutting the tile to the require shape and then honing the surface to make it smooth and remove any saw marks. It is the most smooth and regular finish you can purchase.

Polished

A polished tile is a tile with a flat, even top, straight sides with no edge details and a high sheen to the surface. It is much more common to see polished marble than polished limestone because polishing marble tends to enhance the natural colours and variations in the stone.

The process to create a polished tile is exactly the same as honing except that the surface is honed to a higher degree to create a polished look.

A large honed Sivas floor. You can clearly see the clean, straight edges and the smooth surface of the honed tile. Martin Moore and Co.

A honed, polished limestone in a kitchen. You can clearly see the high sheen and slightly reflective quality of the tiles. Martin Moore and Co.

This aged French limestone is called Aged Gevrey. There are a variety of antiquing treatments for stone. In this example the stone has been pillowed and chiselled on each edge. Martin Moore and Co.

An aged and pillowed Purbeck marble flagstone floor. The grout has been selected to match the lightest colour in the stone.

Traditional Finishes

Aged and Pillowed

This is a hand-finished antiquing process that tends to be carried out on more traditional English and French limestones. The tile is smooth on top with the edges gently rounded and finished with a chisel to give a traditional appearance. It gives a mellow look, which is becoming increasingly popular as clients seek to replicate the worn-smooth look of antique flagstones. An example of an aged and pillowed Gevrey floor is shown in the photo (Gevrey is a limestone from Burgundy in France).

Bersheba is an Israeli limestone. Here the surface of the stone has been wire-brushed to give a textured appearance. This texture gives a non-slip finish. Martin Moore and Co.

These tiles have been tumbled – spun in a large drum – which rounds the edges and lightly textures the top. This tends to be the least expensive way of antiquing stone.
Martin Moore and Co.

This process can also be carried out on traditional English stones, as shown in the aged Farringdon floor photo.

As this process is primarily carried out by hand it does tend to be slightly more expensive than other antiqued finishes.

Brushed

A brushed tile has a textured surface and can sometimes come with chipped edges. This look is created by cutting the tile into the required shape and then brushing the surface with wire brushes to texture it. Some quarries tend to sandblast the tile after it has been brushed to make the surface slightly smoother and more worn. This is a less expensive way of antiquing a tile than the aged and pillowed finish though it tends to give a more rugged appearance.

Tumbled

This tends to be the least expensive antiqued finish and is created entirely by machine. The

This Antique Grey Barr is a reclaimed 18th-century floor from Languedoc in France. Note the textured antique surface of the stone and the large flagstone sizes. Martin Moore and Co.

RIGHT: **Quarrying in the Purbeck Hills in Dorset. The small scale of the quarry is clear from the method of cutting blocks of stone. You can clearly see in the photo the different colour layers of limestone being extracted.**

BELOW: **Cutting the blocks of stone from the quarry wall in a large marble quarry. Once the blocks are cut they will be cut again into scants and then into tiles.**

A traditional English limestone. The stone is cut into random sizes and has been hand-antiqued with pillowed edges.

stone is cut into the required shape and then spun in a machine. This has the effect of rounding the corners and lightly distressing the surface.

This is usually the most cost-effective way of antiquing limestones, travertines and marbles.

Flame-Textured

A flame textured tile is a honed tile cut into regular shapes that then has a naked flame applied to the surface. This has the effect of lightening the colour and providing a texture to the surface. This treatment has become less common over recent years as it tends to be more expensive to produce and can only be used with selected stones – it can only be carried out on very hard stones, primarily limestone, slate and granite.

Riven Finish

A riven finish can be created with certain slates and sandstones. It is achieved by cutting the stone into slabs and simply splitting the stone in half, so is a completely natural finish. However, it is only available with certain stones, most commonly sandstone or slate. The riven finish makes it a very practical choice as a non-slip surface, particularly outdoors.

Antique Reclaimed Stone

It is possible to purchase and use antique reclaimed limestone, terracotta, marble and slate. These are reclaimed materials which are commonly over 200 years old. These create a unique antique appearance but tend to be very expensive. Such material will be thicker and will also vary in size and depth from tile to tile, so you will require a specialist installer if you intend to use it.

There is now a continuous supply of antique French limestone and terracotta. Due to inheritance laws in France older properties tend to change hands much more frequently than in the UK, leading to more salvage of their flooring. There are several reclamation yards in France that have managed to refine these materials to make a reasonably consistent, clean stone.

It is also possible to source a wide range of antique terracotta from France. Materials such as Antique Blanc Rose and Antique Parrefueille tend to have lovely, warm, antique tones that are simply impossible to replicate in modern floors.

Due to the smaller size of the industry in the UK, at the time of writing, antique reclaimed English flooring suppliers tend to offer less refined products. It is common to find Antique Yorkstone, however, which is usually 4–5cm thick and less refined than the French equivalent. It is also less expensive. From time to time it is also possible to find Antique Cotswold and Portland flagstones if one looks hard enough and is patient.

Antique reclaimed flooring can also be sourced from Israel and Belgium.

If you are considering an antique stone it is vitally important to see the batch of stone before delivery. As these materials are in limited supply, the variation between batch to batch in terms of colour and texture is often greater than with recently quarried alternatives.

Antiqued/Second Face Stones

When antique stone is reclaimed it is often 4–5cm thick, which is too thick for modern properties, French and Israeli reclamation yards tend to slice the back of the stone to reduce the antique stone to 2–3cm deep. Over recent years several of these yards have then brushed the bottom of the stone to give a brushed finish while retaining the size and edges of the original antique tile. This is a way of getting a traditional finish for less money than the antique original.

SOURCING STONE – UK VERSUS IMPORTED

Limestone, sandstone and slate have been quarried in the British Isles and used for flooring since Roman times. When you travel around the country you can see many areas where local stones have been used in the construction of historic buildings. Portland stone, and its use in buildings such as Westminster Abbey, is familiar, but there are many other local stones that are less well known: examples of these are Midhurst sandstone in Sussex, Purbeck marble in Dorset and Ancaster in Lincolnshire. Local stones were historically used in their areas and it was possible in travelling across the country to clearly tell the differences.

As the world developed and it became cost-effective to transport heavy goods at low cost across the world the situation changed. Labour costs outside Western Europe are a lot lower and it became possible to supply stone from further afield at a more competitive price than local stones. Most stone retailers now can boast material from far-flung places such as Israel, India and China, among others.

However, the recent cultural shift to a greater interest in environmental issues is causing this to change again. Clients are now concerned with issues such as how far the stone has travelled and the working conditions of the people who have produced it, and are starting actively to look for local stones again. This is leading to increased demand for materials from the UK and is putting pressure on producers to increase quantities produced and lower prices. This situation has of late been assisted by the collapse of the pound against the euro and dollar, making it more expensive to import into the UK. Many people are looking to live in a more sympathetic and less destructive manner with their local environment, and using natural stone flooring from UK producers is certainly the sustainable choice here.

In comparison to other flooring materials stone also stands up as a sustainable choice. Porcelain and ceramics are produced overseas (largely in Spain and Italy) and therefore travel many miles to market to be sold in the UK. There are a whole variety of issues involved in producing wooden flooring, such as responsible forest management. Most of the wood that retails for flooring in the UK is again cut and sourced overseas.

In the past the price put many clients off UK stone, but this is becoming less of an issue. At the time of writing it is quite possible to pick up good-quality English limestone from £65 per square metre plus VAT, while a good porcelain or ceramic will cost at least £50–£55 per square metre plus VAT.

In summary, there are many reasons to choose a UK-sourced stone floor. It will have a natural beauty that fits in the home. It will have been sourced locally, maintaining traditions and an industry that has been running for many years. It will also have a very short journey from production to your home.

At the same time it is important to understand that not all quarries produce to the same quality standards. If you are intending to purchase a UK-sourced stone it is better to visit a retailer who will be able to give you a clear idea on the colour and fossil variation in the stone and will also be able to provide after-sales service should it be needed.

CHAPTER 2

Stone for Different Rooms

It is important to understand the characteristics of the material and its suitability for the area you intend to use it. The range of natural stone is so large that in making a choice you must be guided not only by the aesthetic appearance but also by practicality. This chapter covers the key areas to consider.

FLOORING

It is vital that any flooring material is durable, so it is important to choose the right product. Stone varies in density to a considerable degree. Obviously higher-density stone is more durable and should be used for flooring. Lower-density materials are softer and therefore are more suited to items such as fireplaces and skirtings, as they are easier to carve and to form into shapes. There is a wide range of suitable flooring material available, so check this with your retailer. Generally material from Turkey, Spain and Portugal tends to be lower density and therefore will be harder to clean and look after. Travertine is very cheap but is not suitable for high-density areas. This material naturally has holes in the surface. Quarries will fill the holes with resin (which contributes to the soft, swirly patterns in travertine), but small holes will develop in the stone over time,

Brushed limestone with an open texture. This type of stone will, over time, collect dirt in its open pores unless a treatment is put on it to prevent this.

which will require immediate repair to avoid trapping dirt.

It is also important to consider the practicality of the surface of the stone. If you choose a material with a smooth surface this will be an easy natural stone to look after. If you choose a material that has fossil holes or open veins in the surface these may pick up dirt as people walk over the floor. This is not a failure of the sealer; it is simply dirt from the bottom of people's shoes building up in the holes in the stone. The only cure for this is to put a protective coat of Lilothin Multiseal (or something similar) over the top of the stone. This forms a transparent protective layer over the stone and will stop dirt getting ground into any open fossil holes, but will need to be reapplied every 18–24 months. Alternatively, you can fill the holes with grout upon installation. However, grout will slowly discolour over time and therefore this is not the best option, unless you are content with a more rustic look.

The next section discusses the issues to consider with specific rooms in the home. There is a wide range of natural stone available in the UK in terms of density and durability therefore, it is important to choose the correct material for the correct space.

KITCHEN

From a design point of view, the floor in a kitchen should complement the strongest feature in the design, for example the dark granite worktops, the Aga and so on. This usually means that light-coloured floors (and predominantly limestones) tend to be used.

The kitchen is one of the heavy traffic areas in the home so it is very important to choose a floor that is dense and durable. A denser stone has fewer air pockets, will need less sealer and will be easier to look after. If you mention to any retailer that you require a practical material they

This floor has been selected to match the kitchen – the brown tones in the floor match the teak worktop and the rosewood door furniture. The overall tone of the floor is warm to complement the cream-coloured kitchen. Martin Moore and Co.

A clean, blue/black natural stone used as a kitchen worktop. You can see how the drainer grooves have been cut into the surface and the detail of how it overhangs the sink.

should automatically show you the harder, more practical stones.

While light-coloured floors are common in the kitchen it is sensible to choose a stone with some fossil and variation, because a very clean limestone will show every footprint or dirt mark immediately. There are plenty of light stones available with scattered fossil, which tend to show the dirt less quickly and are easier to look after.

Unless the kitchen is very big it is sensible to choose a regular-size stone pattern (for example 40cm × 60cm or 40cm × random lengths). Most kitchens have narrow spaces and large tiles can look inappropriate – for example, the gap between a kitchen island and the main part of the kitchen is regularly close to 1 metre. If there is just one tile spanning this gap, then this can look wrong with regard to the scale of the room.

Kitchen Worktop

It is possible to use a natural stone for a kitchen top. The most common stones by some distance are granites. These hard, durable stones come in a wide variety of colours. They need to be sealed after installation but after this will provide a durable practical surface that is very easy to maintain and look after, and has always been a popular material in UK homes. If you are considering using a granite it is worth visiting the yard of the granite supplier. Large granite wholesalers will let you look through the slabs they hold in stock so you can easily select the slab you wish to use for your project.

It is possible to use limestones and marbles for kitchen worktops but you need to ensure you select the very hardest material. Limestone or marble can also etch when acid is dropped on

An aged and pillowed Bath stone used as a splashback in a kitchen. This material was chosen to match the floor tile. Martin Moore and Co.

Belgian blue limestone used for kitchen worktops and a bespoke sink. The sink will have been carved from a large block of stone and is an effective centrepiece to the room.

A traditional Victorian decorative design for laying stone in a hallway. One corner has been clipped on every tile and a dark cabochon inserted. A border tile has also been cut from the main field stone on the floor. Martin Moore and Co.

the surface, and acid – in the form of foods such as vinegar or fruit juice – is common in kitchens. If you use the worktop for food preparation, which is likely, there is a risk of etching, and if this happens the worktop cannot be repaired. Granite is always a better choice.

Kitchen Splashback

It is possible to use stone for a kitchen splashback, in both traditional and contemporary schemes. For a traditional scheme it is sensible to keep the same stone for the splashback as was chosen for the floor in smaller tile sizes. This will keep a link to the floor while adapting the scale to the smaller size of the splashback.

It is also possible to use a striking contemporary stone to act as a splashback.

It is important to bear in mind, however, that all types of natural stone are porous and therefore even when used as a splashback they must be sealed properly on installation.

HALLWAY

The hallway is another high-traffic area of the home, so again will require a high-density, durable stone. A denser stone has fewer air pockets, will need less sealer and will be easier to look after. If you decide to look for a light-coloured stone for the hallway it is also sensible to choose a material that has fossil and/or marking, as it will not show the dirt so much when you walk on the floor. It is also wise to incorporate a large inset door mat right behind the front door. If you mention to a retailer that you require a practical material they should automatically start showing you the harder, more practical stones.

As hallways generally have little other furniture it is also possible to make a statement with the floor – for example, by incorporating darker colours.

The photograph on page 41 shows a traditional Victorian hallway floor in stone. This floor has square-cut tiles that have been laid in a diagonal pattern as you enter the space. It has a blue insert tile inserted in one corner of every large square tile, and a thin border laid right around the outside of the space. This is a design that started in Victorian townhouses but has been adapted

to suit many different types of property. If you wanted to adapt this design to a more modern property, for example, you could use large main tiles and keep the insert tile the same material as the main stone.

It is not essential to follow the design shown. It is possible to tile a hallway with a more regular tile if you are looking for a different feel. Most hallways are long and narrow, so when laying a rectangular tile, these should always be laid across the space, as it will make the hall look wider and avoid long grout lines stretching into the next room.

When thinking of the size of the stone it is always wise to look at the narrowest point in the hallway. While it is generally a good idea to choose a big size to create an impressive opening to the home, it also has to work in the narrower areas. The floor will look out of proportion if there is only one large tile with cuts on each side spanning the narrowest part of the hall. The same point applies when deciding whether to incorporate a border into the design. If in the narrowest area, the hall consists of one tile with a border, this will look wrong.

Finally, it is worth pointing out that all natural stones are porous and must be sealed correctly upon installation when used in a hallway. Once the floor is sealed correctly it will be a hard-wearing, durable and practical floor.

BATHROOMS AND TOILETS

As the price of natural stone has fallen over recent years many people now like to use it in the bathroom. Bathrooms tend to get a lot less wear than the kitchen or hall in the average home and therefore it is realistic to look at materials such as premium travertines (or other less dense materials) as practical alternatives for use. They have the added advantage of being less expensive than granite, limestone or marble.

As most bathrooms have little natural light it is always best to choose a light-coloured material with a bit of movement or variation in the surface. This provides visual interest but will give a soft, cosy feel to the room. This is another reason that travertine is a popular choice for bathrooms.

The major issue for the floor is whether to choose a simple honed tile or to select a material

A standard honed travertine tile installed with a matching travertine dado rail. This provides a simple but effective method to make a break between the tiles and the painted wall. Martin Moore and Co.

A large bathroom where the scheme centres around the large, white, free-standing bath. The walls are painted, except for a built-in shelf, which is fitted with mosaic.

The walls of this shower area have been fitted with rectangular tiles, which has the effect of stretching the width of the wall and making the space look larger.

that has been lightly antiqued (for example, tumbled or brushed) to give a practical, non-slip surface.

Bathroom Walls

It is also possible to tile bathroom walls in stone. The client has to decide between the following options:

- **To tile all walls from floor to ceiling.** The advantage of doing this is it keeps the same theme throughout the room. However, it is sensible to consider adding a mosaic border (widely available) or some kind of moulded dado rail (as shown in the photograph) to break up the wall of stone. If a mosaic is chosen this can be in the same stone or in something complementary.
- **To tile all walls from floor to dado rail height.** The advantage of doing this is that it allows the homeowner to decorate the rest of the room as they wish. In the photo you can see a travertine wall tile taken up to dado rail height and finished with a moulded travertine dado rail. In this instance the client decided to paint the walls white and hang pictures to give a light, homely feel.
- **To tile only one wall floor to ceiling.** This approach is known as creating a feature wall and is particularly appropriate if you want to use a darker and more striking stone or mosaic design in the bathroom. The best approach is to choose the largest, most visible wall that you see when you enter the bathroom. It is also possible to choose a very neutral stone for the floor to complement the feature wall and make it the main focus of the room.

With regard to size it is generally sensible to use square tiles on the floor with rectangular tiles on the walls. This appears to stretch the walls and make what is often a small room seem larger and more luxurious.

LEFT: **A typical Indian stone that is used outside. It has a non-slip surface and textured edges.**

BELOW: **A variety of different uses for stone in a garden – it has been used for the floor and for the terracing.**

EXTERNAL USE

It is vitally important if you intend to fit a natural stone tile outside in the UK that you check that it is frost-resistant. Material that is not frost resistant will suffer from frost heave. This means that water will collect in open pores in the stone. This will freeze when the temperature drops and the surface of the stone will begin to flake away. This is irreversible and cannot be repaired. A competent retailer will be able to direct you to frost-resistant stone. There is a wide range of Indian sandstone on the market in the UK that is both inexpensive and frost-resistant. This tends to be the most common material in use for external terraces, though you can also use a variety of slates or limestones. It is vitally important that whatever material you choose for external use has a riven or aged surface so that it has a non-slip surface.

It is also important, when laying external stone in the UK, that the patio or terrace is laid with a fall – that is, on a slight angle so rain water is never sitting directly on the stone and is always able to run off onto the lawn. This will allow proper drainage and will reduce the chance of any algae or moss growing on the patio.

The depth of the stone that you choose is very important and depends on the base that you have chosen. If you are laying on sand and cement you must use a stone that is at least 3cm thick. A concrete base gives a firmer foundation so you can choose a thinner stone, but it is important to seek advice from the company who supplies the stone about what is suitable and what is not.

CHAPTER 3

Floors

MATCHING TRADITIONAL STONE FLOORS

If you live in an older property in certain parts of the UK it is very possible that you may have an old stone floor or stone feature (such as a stone fireplace, windowsills and so on) that you may wish to match in your new stone floor. As many of the active quarries have been working for hundreds of years this is normally possible. For example, many parts of central London and other cities use Portland stone. There are also areas of the country where the building stock is almost exclusively the local natural stone, for example the honey-coloured local stone from the Cotswolds, the light grey limestone from Bath and the sandy-coloured limestone from Lincolnshire. There are also several regions where slate has been used extensively for flooring for hundreds of years, such as the Lake District, west Wales and Caithness. It is also possible to source Yorkstone, which has been used extensively internally and externally across the UK.

If you wish to use a local stone in your property (without matching it to an existing stone floor) this is fairly straightforward – it is simply a case of examining the local buildings, or alternatively asking a local builder or stonemason about local stone that was historically used in the area. From this point it is relatively simple to find out if it can still be sourced. It is worth checking the durability of the stone currently produced. For example, a lot of older properties in Sussex and Surrey traditionally used Horsham and Midhurst sandstone, which is a very porous material and not really suited for modern flooring. If you live in this area and wish to incorporate this stone, it is wiser to

use it for a fireplace, a fire hearth or a windowsill and use something similar but more durable for the floor.

If your intention is to try to match a historic floor, this can be a more complicated process but is still possible. Much will depend on the material you are trying to match. Portland has historically been used across central and west London (the Bank of England and St Paul's Cathedral are built from Portland stone). Cotswold limestone was historically used for the interiors of many of the great houses of middle England. Bath stone has been a building stone used across the southwest since Roman times. There are other historic limestones still in production today, for example Lincolnshire limestone, Purbeck limestone and Forest of Dean limestone.

It will be very difficult for light limestones to gain an exact match to an older floor. The reasons for this are twofold. Even if you are able to identify the source and type of stone on the floor and the quarry is still working, it will be in a completely different part of the quarry wall and therefore the material will look different. Also, it is simply not possible to replicate how the stone will have worn over the period of time that it has been in your property. The best course of action is often to source the same stone but in a different size and finish. This will link the two areas of flooring but will also make it obvious that the new floor is not trying to imitate the original but is trying sympathetically to complement it.

With darker materials such as Yorkstone or slate the chances of getting a good match are much higher. Yorkstone can be sourced as an antique reclaimed floor. If you have a house with an old riven flagstone floor with grey-green tones it is very likely Yorkstone. The best way to source this material is to visit a big local reclamation yard. They will have material that has been reclaimed from local properties, so this is your best chance of getting something with the right finish and size. If you cannot obtain a good match from a reclamation yard then the best option may be to take a similar approach to that outlined above for light-coloured limestones. Yorkstone today is produced in a wide variety of quarries across Yorkshire and Derbyshire and therefore it is fairly easy to find a tone that will be sympathetic to the original floor.

If you are trying to match old slate flagstones this is more straightforward. The major point to consider is ensuring the best match of finish. Once this has been done it is simply a case of getting the best colour match possible.

It is generally a good idea if extending any stone floor to have the original stone floor stripped, cleaned and resealed at the time of installation. This will give you the best chance of getting a good colour match. It will also mean that the practical maintenance of the area should be straightforward as both floors will need treating and resealing at the same time.

If there are any architectural details in your property it may be worth considering them when thinking about the choice of stone. For example, distinctive covings can be copied in the design of a fireplace mantle. If you are putting in a stone skirting the detail should match the existing wooden or stone skirting in the property. If you are installing a stone staircase you should think of matching the edge detail to the front of the treads to the style of other existing staircases or steps within the property.

The final point to make in this section is to emphasize the importance of keeping a few spare tiles when you choose and install a new floor. Should you then decide to extend the floor at some future point you will have tiles you can carry with you and give to potential suppliers, which will make the process of choosing a material much simpler.

TOWN OR COUNTRY

Stone floors can be really helpful in setting the

Here the edge detail of the skirting has been selected to match the edge details of the tread on the staircase. This a simple way of building links between the pieces of stone to link the design.

atmosphere for any room in the home. We covered in the previous section the reasons for sourcing local stone for your property. Aside from this, stone can also be used to create a rustic or contemporary look as desired.

Rustic Look

If you are aiming for a rustic look, this can be best achieved in a floor by sourcing large, flagstone-shaped tiles, either in a mixture of lengths (for example 40cm × random lengths) or uniform size (for example, 50cm × 70cm). If at the same time you source a material that is local to the area or looks traditional this will also help. Other points to be considered are possibly applying a coat of wax to the floor and keeping the grout lines at 4–5mm.

You do not necessarily need to source a UK stone to get a rustic look – most retailers stock

An aged and pillowed Bath stone floor laid in a traditional 40 × random lengths pattern to give a rustic look. Martin Moore and Co.

a range of imported stones that are antiqued and will be a lot less expensive than home-quarried natural stones. As there are now many different ways of antiquing stone this allows you quite a bit of choice over how the stone is finished, though it is important to ensure that the stone you choose is antiqued in some way to obtain that rustic look.

Contemporary Look

If you are going for a contemporary look, this is best achieved by sourcing large honed tiles (60cm × 60cm or larger) and installing these tiles with the tightest grout joint possible (2–3mm). You should carefully select the grout so that it matches the lightest colour in the stone.

It is also worth considering the current trends for colours when choosing a material. At the time of writing the colour of choice for contemporary interiors is clean, clinical white. As there are

no UK-sourced white or off-white stones, achieving the most contemporary look will generally involve choosing a stone sourced from the developing world. This has the advantage that it will generally be less expensive than something sourced in the UK. Obviously, it is important that any stone chosen for a contemporary look is installed in a honed finish to give the crispest appearance possible.

PERIOD HOUSES

If you are restoring a period house it is worth considering how the floors would have been displayed. It was during the Georgian and Victorian eras that ideas of decorating the home first gained ground among the British people. This is when you start seeing schemes like the hallway shown in the photo, with square tiles laid in a diagonal pattern

A contemporary limestone floor called St Aubin, which is quarried in Germany. Here it is in a honed format. Martin Moore and Co.

with a dark inset tile. If you wish to copy this look it is not important to use the same stones.

Before the Victorian era the interiors of homes were determined by more practical considerations. In the Tudor period the floor was generally supplied by the nearest local quarry and the size pattern was decided by the mason on site installing the floor breaking the tiles where he could into the most regular sizes. Thus the floor in a 16th-century country cottage in the Chiltern Hills would have a completely different floor style than the floors in a 19th-century Victorian townhouse. It is important to understand this if you are trying to add stone to your property in a manner sympathetic to the original building.

It is always a good idea to look through copies of the latest interior design magazines to get an idea of the look you want to achieve, whether town or country. There are plenty to choose from, such as *House and Garden*, *Homes and Gardens*, *Country Living* and *Country Life*. These magazines will be very helpful in showing which paint colours and other finishes will work with a particular stone floor.

With the range of natural stones on the market there will be plenty of choice across the price range to suit any budget and also obtain any look.

WHERE TO BUY A STONE FLOOR

There are now several different routes to source a natural stone floor, listed below with their advantages and disadvantages

Over the Internet
Over recent years various sites have sprung up advertising natural stone over the internet. There are several things to consider if you are thinking of buying via the internet:

- You may get a better price for a known material.
- You cannot see what you will get so you have to be certain of the variation of the material you have purchased.
- Most internet retailers are based at warehouses in a specific location in the country, so if aftersales help is needed it may be many miles away.

If you know exactly what material you need, it may be possible to purchase it at a better price over the internet than direct from a showroom, but there are risks to this method of purchasing a floor, which should be understood before proceeding down this route.

Direct From a Quarry
It is possible to buy stone direct from some quarries. If you know what you want, it is possible to obtain a better price by buying direct but there are several points to bear in mind:

- It is difficult to understand the range and variation of what you will get unless you can see a large display floor.
- Quarries are set up to deal with trade retailers and therefore aftersales service is generally not to the same standard as a retailer's.
- Some quarries produce very good-quality finished products while other quarries produce very poor-quality products. To buy direct from a quarry you must have a clear understanding of how to tell a well-finished stone floor from a poor one.

From a Retailer
There are a range of retailers across the country who offer natural stone floors to the public. The key issues to consider here are:

- It is advisable to shop around to ensure you get the best price. Many retailers offer a similar range of products at very varied prices. The national retailers in particular tend to be more expensive than more local chains.
- You will get the opportunity with most retailers to see a large display floor, which will give you some idea of the range of colour, veins and fossils that you will get in your floor.
- A retailer will also be able to give you specialist advice on the best floor to suit your particular needs.
- A retailer will in general offer a better level of aftersales service than you would receive buying direct from a quarry or via the internet.

The aim of this section is not to recommend one route of buying a floor over another. It is simply to give the reader the relevant information to enable them to understand the strengths and weaknesses of each particular way of buying a stone floor. Informed choices generally lead to the best decisions.

Selecting a Stone From Samples

It is very important when selecting a stone to see a big display, preferably in a retailer's showroom.

Stone is a natural material and does vary in colour from batch to batch. Some people try to make decisions from small samples and this can be very dangerous as it will give no hint of the variety of colours and features that may appear in the floor. It is also important to ask the retailer if the display floor you are looking at is an accurate reflection of how the material currently looks. Any competent retailer will show a big display and will also be happy to lend you full size tiles to look at in your home.

SIZE OF TILE

One of the most important aspects in choosing a floor is to select the right tile size. It is now

An upmarket stone retail showroom. When visiting a showroom you need to be certain you are seeing a good display of each stone so that you understand the variation.

Aged Gevrey limestone laid in a large repeat random pattern. The grout has been selected to match the lightest colours present in the stone.

The large 60cm × 60cm tile fitted into the floor of this bathroom give it a clean, modern look.

possible to buy most stone tiles in at least three or four sizes. Choosing the right size can help to add the final detail to the project.

There are several standard patterns of flooring. Some of the most popular are listed below:

40cm × 40cm This is a square tile. This size is most popular in more modern schemes or areas where space is limited.

40cm × 60cm This is the most popular size, produced by all large quarries. It is the most versatile size and can be used in many different spaces.

40cm × random length This size is trying to replicate a more traditional size of flooring. The tiles have a fixed width of 40cm but the length is completely random. The advantage of this size is that with most stones it is the most economical to produce, as the quarry can use a block of any size and saw all the way through it; there is less waste and therefore the production cost is lower.

50cm × random length Same as the above but slightly wider.

Repeat random patterns There are a variety of repeat random patterns available, the most common of which is known as Roman Opus. This is a repeat pattern consisting of four interlocking tiles, mimicking completely random antique floors of the past. The disadvantage of this pattern is that it tends to have some small sizes and therefore is not best over large areas.

60cm × 60cm This is the most popular size for a contemporary modern project. It is a large square tile which is most effective used in a very clean stone floor with little variation. It tends to be slightly more expensive than a 40cm × 40cm or 40cm × 40cm tile.

The smaller tiles in this random-length floor were deliberately positioned between the kitchen cupboards and the island to make this gap look larger. Martin Moore and Co.

Large St Luke tiles give a clean, contemporary look to this large, modern kitchen.
Martin Moore and Co.

Most suppliers will offer tiles in different sizes to those detailed above – for example, it is possible to obtain natural stone floors in large sizes (such as 80cm × 80cm, 90cm × 90cm and so on), although larger size tiles will generally be on special order from the quarry and therefore will be on longer lead times. It should also be noted that as they are too large to be cut on a standard tile production line they will also be more expensive.

Grout Joints

A key point that governs the final appearance of any stone floor is setting the grout joint to the right size. The traditional rule has always been

that if you are looking for contemporary look you should set the grout joint as close as possible. Due to the thickness of the saw used for cutting stone tiles there will always be a slight margin of error with the size of the tiles, so the closest it is practically possible to lay tiles is generally 2–3mm.

If you are trying to create a rustic look the grout line should be wider but not too wide. The ideal grout joint for a rustic floor is 4–5mm.

It is worth noting that if you choose a repeat random pattern floor, most patterns are not designed to give the same grout joint size. This is not necessarily a problem as the aim of these patterns is to create a rustic look. It is common with a repeat random pattern floor to have a grout line between 4mm and 6 mm in the same floor.

The important thing to remember when considering which size tile to purchase is that every project is different and that the decision on the size of tile will be determined by the size and shape of the room, the amount of furniture and the aesthetic preferences of the person choosing the floor. Below are three examples of real-life different situations and the factors considered in each scenario.

Scenario 1 – Farmhouse Kitchen

This project comprised a kitchen 8.5m long and 5m wide in a farmhouse. The client was searching for a rustic look for the floor and chose an aged and pillowed Farringdon limestone, sourced from the Purbeck Hills in Dorset. The kitchen was an L-shape design with a large island in the middle. Large areas of the kitchen floor were visible.

The client was keen to maintain a rustic look to the property and liked the appearance of traditional flagstones. We discussed using a repeat random pattern but the client took the view that this kind of pattern tends to have some small tiles in it. We discussed using a tile with a fixed width and variable lengths; however, the client felt this did not have enough variety of pattern. The final decision was to use a floor made up of tiles 40cm, 50cm and 60cm wide and completely random lengths. Due to the size of the room it was possible for the large sizes in the floor to be seen. The tiler selected some of the smaller lengths and laid them between the kitchen and island, which had the added advantage of making this gap look larger due to the number of tiles used.

Scenario 2 – Contemporary Townhouse

This project was in a large London home. The client chose Steinach, which is a light-grey stone with clumps of large fossil. The space involved was over 100sq m, and the client was keen to have as large a stone as possible. We decided that 40cm × 40cm was too small and the client finally chose a 60cm × 80cm tile. It was fitted with a neutral grout, which blended in with the background colour of the stone. This worked well in the space and gave the appearance of one continuous large stone floor. The 60cm × 80cm size was chosen rather than 60cm x 60cm as this mimicked the shape of the room. The chosen tile was a strong colour, and the colours in the kitchen were then chosen to complement the floor.

Scenario 3 – Victorian Hallway

This client wanted to lay a traditional hallway in a large Victorian townhouse in Wandsworth, south London. The hall was narrow at the front yet opened up into a larger area at the foot of the stairwell. The decision was taken to go for 40cm × 40cm tiles. The reason for this was the narrowest part of the hall was 1.3m wide, so if 60cm × 60cm tiles had been chosen, two tiles would have spanned the hall. The client wanted to make the hall look wider and therefore smaller tiles were better. The client wanted to use cabochons in the traditional Victorian style, and to avoid the floor looking like a grid the 40cm × 40cm tile was turned onto the diagonal. This also allowed space to incorporate a 10cm-wide border to each side, which flowed throughout the space and wrapped around the bottom of the staircase. This made the hall look grander in the manner the house deserved.

CHAPTER 4

Architectural Stone

KITCHENS

For many years it has been common practice to use stone for countertops in UK homes. It provides a natural warmth and colour as well as a practical surface that is easy to look after.

Worktops and Sinktops

Most mid-range to upmarket kitchens in the UK have granite worktops and splashbacks. Granite is the most durable of natural stones and, after sealing, is a very practical material for the kitchen. It does not pick up water marks, is virtually impossible to stain and is heat-resistant. No other natural material can boast these characteristics. It also comes in big slabs, which means large areas of furniture can be covered in one piece of stone. Granite also offers lots of design choices due to the wide variety of colours available, ranging from consistent dark blue and black shades through to striking light-coloured stones full of movement and colour.

The texture of the stone also contributes to the overall appearance. Apart from the easily recognizable polished finish, granite tops can be found in honed, brushed and flamed finishes. The clean contemporary polished finish is perceived as elegant and formal whereas the honed finish is often chosen by those seeking a more casual and relaxed ambience.

If you are planning to choose a granite for a

A kitchen with a Belgian blue granite top. The granite top is 30mm thick and has been finished with a double pencil round edge.

- **Edge detail.** There is a vast array of different edge details that can be applied to a kitchen worktop. The most common finish in the UK is the double pencil round. Obviously the more detailed and ornate the edge, the more expensive it is to produce.
- **Sink cutouts.** If a sink cutout is required this will add to the cost. If the sink is slung on top of the worktop, the saw cut does not need to be polished and this reduces cost. If the sink is underslung, however, the sink cutout does need to be polished, which is additional work and therefore will cost more.
- **Drainer grooves.** If drainer grooves are required to both sides of the sink this is additional work, which again adds to cost; however, this will stop water pooling on top of the worktop.
- **Thickness of the worktop.** The common depth for kitchen worktops in the UK is 30mm, although more contemporary designs generally use a 50mm-thick piece of stone. While this looks impressive, you are obviously using 60 per cent more stone, which has an effect on cost. Some clients choose to use 20mm-thick stone, as this reduces the cost.

Seal all stone surfaces with an impregnating sealant to ensure a practical and hardwearing surface.

An installation where the same stone has been used for the worktop and for the floor. Note the overslung sink.

kitchen worktop it is worth visiting a large granite wholesaler so that you can pick the individual slab you wish to use.

Limestone and marble are used less frequently in the UK as they are prone to marking from acids, which are commonly found in the kitchen in ingredients such as red wine, fruit juice and some fruits and vegetables. Bizarrely, limestone and marble are very common as worktops in mainland Europe.

A good proportion of the cost of a kitchen worktop is based on the amount of work that is required to prepare the stone. Key elements of cost tend to be:

Ideas for Kitchen Design

- Dark granites tend to be the dominant feature in the kitchen and therefore it is wise to choose paints and decorative features to complement them.
- Mix and match slabs – you can really add to a design by using a couple of different materials – for example, granite for the central island and a different stone elsewhere.
- Consider using stone for the splashback. It can be a cost-effective and striking way to improve the design. Install the worktop first and the splashback second to ensure a watertight seal.
- If you are aiming for a traditional look, consider making the chimney section in the kitchen from traditional stone, such as Bath stone.

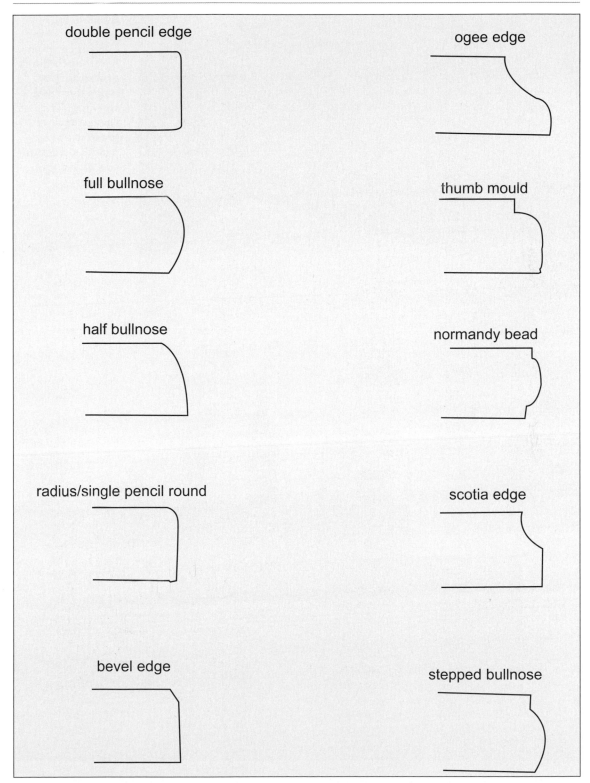

double pencil edge

ogee edge

full bullnose

thumb mould

half bullnose

normandy bead

radius/single pencil round

scotia edge

bevel edge

stepped bullnose

Edge details, suitable for stone 2–3cm thick.

Small details can make all the difference when it comes to the practicality of stone used as a worktop. The carved drainer grooves are a practical addition to this granite top.

This picture shows how easy it is to make an effective shelf in any room of the house with stone. In this example pieces of granite have made a simple shelf for condiments in a kitchen.

ABOVE: **A bathroom countertop made out of calico marble. Note the upstand and mirror frame made from the same material.**

RIGHT: **The same countertop photographed from further back. You can see how slabs of marble have been fitted round the top of the walnut cupboard as a design feature.**

BATHROOMS

Over recent years there has been an increasing trend to the use of natural stone slabs in the bathroom. The reasons are many. As some stones have come down in price so have the slab prices, and therefore this smart, elegant way of finishing the bathroom has become more affordable. Many bathrooms have little natural light, which leads towards choosing light materials with colour and variation.

The most popular materials for bathrooms tend to be limestone, travertine or marble. Limestone tends to have the least variation, and if a look is sought where the tops or walls are a close match to the floor tile, this is the best choice. Travertine

A moulded travertine dado rail used as a capping piece to finish off a tile.

is very common. It is the least expensive natural stone and the elegant swirly patterns within the stone lend themselves to creating a warm and welcoming earthy feel in the bathroom. Marble is the most striking of these three stones and tends to be used only on the most contemporary projects. Marble slabs are also more difficult to match to the tiles chosen due to the greater variation in the stone.

All of these three stones can be sourced in mosaic form or with a series of pre-cut borders, which can provide a very effective complement to the tiles as a border, shower wall or other decorative feature.

There are a wide variety of moulded dado rails, mosaics and similar stone details that can be purchased for use in bathrooms. As these tend to be manufactured in the quarry they are not expensive and can be a very effective way of adding detail to a bathroom.

Countertops

If there are any countertops in your bathroom this is another opportunity to use a natural stone. Most of the main travertines, marbles and limestones are available in slab and can be easily worked to make countertops, bath tops or shelves. If you wish to incorporate a darker stone in the bathroom another way of doing this is to use it for one or all of the tops.

Going for a 20mm-deep slab is the most cost-effective way of installing a stone worktop in the bathroom, though a 30mm slab will look a lot more substantial and visually impressive.

Showers, Baths and Sinks

Natural stone can also be used if you are planning a walk-in shower area or wet room. It is important to allow for the shower/wet room floor to be sloped towards a drain in the centre of the floor so that no water is left sitting on the surface of the stone.

Pre-made shower trays can be bought off the shelf from a variety of retailers. These are normally made from travertine, a stone that can be particularly effective in a shower. As they are mass produced they are also fairly price competitive. This kind of product needs to be viewed, and if you are considering purchasing a stone shower tray you should visit a local showroom to gain a full understanding of how it will look.

If you wish to have a bespoke shower tray made this will cost more money as it will be a one-off piece from a quarry. The advantage is that you will have many more options in terms of design and the choice of stone.

In recent years it has also become possible to source solid stone sinks and baths for a truly luxurious bathroom. These are cut straight from block and are therefore more costly than ceramic equivalents, as well as being heavier.

Some retailers offer an off-the-shelf range of travertine bowls that can be added to a bathroom inexpensively.

If you wish to use a stand-alone stone bath these are normally made from travertine and are truly luxurious, albeit very heavy. At the time of writing it is necessary in most properties to strengthen the bathroom floor to allow for a stone bath. They are also far to heavy for manual

Ideas for Bathroom Design Using Stone

- Consider using a smaller, square tile on the floor with larger rectangular tiles on the walls.
- Consider using a clear glass door to a shower or wet room to show off any mosaic or stone designs within the space.
- Consider using a tumbled mosaic on the shower floor as it is totally non clip.
- Avoid polished limestone or marble in the shower as the acidity in some shampoos will eventually strip the sheen from the tile.
- If specifying a dark stone in the bathroom, use it solely for one feature (for example, the vanity top) to enhance the impact.
- It can be an effective idea to make a shelf out of stone to hold things such as shampoo and soap.
- Ensure that any area where water will fall on the stone has adequate drainage so that standing water is not left on the stone.

be clad to the concrete and cut and shaped to fit treads and risers. A wide variety of edge details can be applied to the treads, but it is important to match the detail on the edge of the string to the tread detail.

ABOVE: **You can see the 30mm-thick tread and faceted riser on this curved step.** Stoneclassics

BELOW: **Here you can see how the treads have been lined up to achieve the strongest visual appearance. The landing plate has been made from one large piece of stone.** Stoneclassics

lifting and the normal way to get one into a bathroom is to make a hole in the wall or roof and lift it in by crane. These constraints make a stone bath an unrealistic option for most people.

It is worth noting again that any natural stone chosen for the bathroom will be porous and must be sealed correctly upon installation. However once sealed correctly natural stone will be a practical, hardwearing surface and easy to maintain surface in a bathroom

STAIRCASES

There is nothing as grand or visually impressive as a stone staircase. It can be a classic feature for a hallway and the design centrepiece for your home. The wide availability of slab in many materials means there is a wide variety of both stone and finishes to choose from. To use stone on a staircase it is important to have a firm, hard base – this generally means a concrete base. Stone can then

Stone can easily be adapted to suit curves on treads. The traditional way to do this is to template the top of the step and ask a fabricator to make it into the required shape. In the photos below you can see examples of this.

Ideas for Staircase Design

- While ornate edge details can look good, consider how practical they are for day to day use.
- If using an antiqued stone for a step, bear in mind that any area where the stone has been worked (such as the edge details) will be smooth.
- Thicker treads (for example, 30mm) will look more visually impressive for a front-on view. You can keep costs down by making the riser thinner.
- Steel handrails tend to complement stone staircases very effectively.
- Consider using downlighters to give the staircase a dramatic effect.

ABOVE: **This is the most cost-effective way to fit a riser under a curved stone tread. The stone has been cut into smaller straight sections, which are then fitted together to make a curve. This is a lot less expensive than carving the riser from a solid piece of stone.**

Steinach limestone in use as a staircase. The treads, which are the thicker pieces of stone horizontal to the floor, have been finished with a detailed edge.

FIREPLACES

Nothing is quite as effective a centrepiece to a living room as an imposing stone fireplace. This charismatic detail is now a cross between a luxurious piece of artwork and a stunning piece of furniture.

Once an essential item to heat the home, the fireplace has changed to become a design feature for dining rooms or living rooms and sets the mood for that space. There are many fireplace designs on the market in the UK, ranging from traditional Victorian white marble designs to sand-stone or limestone fireplaces from Tudor or Georgian times. Many are influenced by the designs of world-famous architects and craftsmen such as Robert Adam.

Downlighters can be used to very effectively to create a dramatic effect over a stone staircase.

A modern reworking of a classic bolection style. This has been carved from travertine to give it a more contemporary feel. Martin Moore and Co.

It is also possible to source more modern designs inspired by such diverse influences as the art deco movement or Le Corbusier.

Fireplaces are most commonly seen in a living room. However, they can work very effectively in a kitchen and are commonly seen in bedrooms in Victorian houses.

Once you have looked round a few showrooms you will notice that many of the designs are similar, making it easy to compare prices in order to get the best deal.

The key thing that governs the options for the fireplace is the opening size. If the opening size is smaller than wanted you should ask a builder if it is possible to enlarge it. This can sometimes be done by lifting the lintel on top of the opening. If this is not an option then the fireplace

TOP: **Robert Adam was a designer who lived and worked during the 19th century. You can see examples of his work in many of the great houses of England. This is a traditional Adam fireplace design.** Martin Moore and Co.

LEFT: **This is an example of a traditional, simple Victorian-style fireplace, which was common across the UK. It is shown here in a white marble with a honed black slate hearth.** Martin Moore and Co.

This is a modern reworking of a traditional bolection fireplace design in a French limestone. Slips have been inserted to reduce the size of the fireplace to the opening size. Martin Moore and Co.

size can be adjusted by fitting slips to the inside of the fireplace. These are rectangular pieces of the stone that sit between the fireplace opening and the inside of the fireplace legs. It is customary to fit slips in the same material as the fireplace itself. In some cases, for example when installing a Robert Adam-style marble fireplace, clients choose to supply slips in darker marble but this is quite unusual.

When selecting a fireplace you need to consider whether you want to have a hearth and how you want to dress the inside of the fireplace. Options generally include painting the inside of the hearth with a fireproof paint, or using a stone, cast iron or vermiculite lining. This choice is generally based on the aesthetic look that is wanted as much as the practical needs. If you want a black interior you will need to paint the fireplace or fit a black lining. Sometimes you will be constrained by the opening. If the sides and back of the opening are straight the easiest way to apply a lining is to fit a piece of cast iron or vermiculite. If the back and sides of the opening are not straight then the only option may be to paint the opening. If you decide to fit a stone lining (especially if you have chosen to use a light limestone or marble) be aware that if you have a real fire it may darken the sides of the lining over time. This will be a positive thing if you are trying to create a rustic look but may not be so desirable if you prefer a pristine look.

The Hearth

Another important choice is what material to use for the hearth. The hearth is the piece of stone the fireplace sits upon. It is generally divided into the inner hearth (which is inside the opening) and the outer hearth. It is a good idea to make the outer hearth out of two or three bits of stone to allow for the expansion that will inevitably occur as the fireplace heats and contracts. The most common choices for fireplace hearths are limestone, black granite, black slate or marble. Each has their own characteristics:

Limestone
- It will match the colour of the fireplace.
- A wider variety of colours are available.
- It will show dirt if you are using an open fire from deposits that drop on it.

Slate
- It will give a matt black look, which can complement a white marble or light limestone fireplace effectively.
- Slate is prone to scratching from fireplace tools and similar items. If you want a hearth that will stay in the condition it was installed, this is not the best material.
- It does not get stained or marked by deposits from open fires being dropped on it.

Black Granite
- It can give you a dark consistent look without the maintenance worries of slate.

Ideas for Fireplace Design

- All fireplaces must be sealed to prevent staining of the stone. If you do not seal the stone it will pick up stains from any liquids that are spilled on the fireplace. Many people have a habit of putting drinks on fireplace mantelpieces and therefore it is important to protect it from unwanted incursions.
- Choose a design that suits the style and period of your property. A country cottage will generally require a smaller, more rustic fireplace. In a townhouse it will be more appropriate to go for a cleaner, simpler style.
- The fireplace will become the centrepiece of the space and therefore you should select other materials to complement it. Think about the stone you intend to choose and what colours will complement it.
- Consider what fire you will have in the fireplace when selecting a stone. If you intend to burn coal or wood, a light-coloured limestone hearth will be high-maintenance. Slate is prone to scratching so is not ideal if you are planning to keep ornaments or fire tools on the hearth.
- Adapt the height of the fireplace mantel to suit the floor-to-ceiling height in the room. If you have high ceilings you should make the mantel taller to suit. The fireplace will be the centre of the room.

Ideas for Incorporating Mosaics into a Design

Here you can see how the addition of a small piece of complementary mosaic to a sunken shelf helps the overall design.

- You do not need a lot of mosaic material to make a big impact with design.
- Consider using an aged or tumbled mosaic stone to create a softer feel to the space.
- Mosaic can be equally effective as a border or a design feature, such as a shower wall.
- Mosaic borders are normally most effective when combined with a light stone.
- It is wise to match the finish on a complementary stone to the mosaic tile.
- If using a mosaic as a centrepiece, choose all other materials to complement it as the focal point of the design.

The mosaic floor and wall make a stunning addition to the shower alongside the clean, contemporary marble, and provide a focus for this space.

Ideas for Wine Cellar Design

- Consider using earthy-coloured stone to create the right ambience in the room.
- As the room will have little natural light, consider using lighter-coloured materials.

- It will give you a dark look that complements white marble/light limestone perfectly.
- It is generally more expensive than slate.
- Slate is generally available in larger sizes than black granite.

It is a good idea to apply a pencil round to the front of the hearth so that if it gets knocked by a vacuum cleaner or something similar it will not chip. It is customary to fit the hearth in 5cm depth so that it looks substantial and visually impressive.

WINE ROOMS

Natural stone is a very effective material to use for a wine room. Stone is naturally a conductor and will sit at room temperature, making it perfect to use for a space such as a wine room.

You can easily create the effect of a traditional wine cellar by using materials such as stone, masonry and wood. Consider using the masonry on the wall with a traditional aged stone floor with the fixtures and fitting being wood.

MOSAICS AND MURALS

Mosaic has been used since Roman times as decorative stone, and the basic concept behind it has not changed since then. Small pieces (tesserae) of decorative and aged stone are applied to a mesh and fixed to the floor. They can be supplied in borders, accents, medallions and decorative centrepieces. There is a variety of pre-made designs available, which are the most cost-effective way of buying mosaic. You can also find a mosaic artist to create luxury bespoke mosaics to fit your design brief.

The reader now has all the relevant information to identify the right material for their project, in the right size and the right finish to achieve the desired result. The next section examines how to ensure that the installation process is as smooth as possible.

PART II

Installation

Now that you have chosen the material, decided on the size and design of your stone feature and ordered the relevant materials, it is time to install it.

This section will first look at all the issues involved in installing a stone floor. It will examine the skills needed to do the work, list the tools that are required and then walk step by step through the process, from setting out the room and checking the material that has been delivered right through to the final cleaning of the fitted floor. It will discuss the materials needed to fit the floor, including adhesives, grouts and sealers. The troubleshooting section lists the most common problems with fitted stone floors and how to resolve them.

Specialist techniques for installation of natural stone on walls and outside are also covered, as is the installation of more decorative pieces of natural stone such as mosaic as well as worktops, upstands, stair treads and fireplaces. Finally, there is an extensive glossary defining all the major terms.

CHAPTER 5

Fitting a Stone Floor

Installing a stone floor is not a straightforward task but is something that can be carried by a good tradesman who is prepared to follow a process step by step in a professional manner. However, it should be added that the majority of problems with stone floors are caused by poor installation and basic errors, so if you are going to install your own floor you should make sure you take your time, take things step by step and – most importantly – follow the instructions. If you are not certain of any point you should consult the retailer of the stone or the manufacturer of the specialist product you are dealing with.

Even if you believe you are good with your hands, and you already have experience of installing ceramic tiles, it is essential to pick up a book on laying a natural stone floor to ensure you are familiar with all the basic issues.

If you are considering doing it yourself you should be aware that laying natural stone is a hard physical job. It will test your back, hands and knees, and if you have problems with any of these body parts this may be worth reconsidering.

Stone is also heavier than ceramic tiles. The average 40cm × 60cm tile will weigh approximately 15kg, and the average floor of approximately 40sq m will involve handing 160 tiles. Laying a stone floor is a more intricate, more time-consuming and more detailed job than laying a ceramic floor.

The intention of this section is not to put off the reader but to ensure that the task is undertaken with realistic expectations. If your confidence is high and you wish to proceed, then the first stage is to put together a list of the tools you will need to carry out the job.

TOOLS

This section lists the key tools that will be needed to lay the average stone floor.

Angle grinder. This is a hand-held, high-speed tool that looks like a buffer but has a diamond-tipped wheel instead. The tool is used to make intricate cuts in the stone that would be to difficult to make on the traditional deck wet saw. A grinder for cutting natural stone is normally fitted with a 4in diamond-tipped blade. It can also be used to shape and apply details to exposed tile edges.

Back brace. Laying a stone floor is a physical job. Even if you are in perfect physical health it is sensible to take steps to maintain this position. It is very important (given the weight of stone tiles) to ensure that you are lifting correctly, and a few simple precautions, such as wearing a back brace, should be considered.

Grout joint spacers. These are available in a variety of sizes and are used to maintain a precise grout joint between the tiles. When laying a stone floor the ideal size to use is a 3mm spacer.

Grout sponges. This is a sponge designed for cleaning grouts and adhesive from a tile's surface (which, if left behind, will leave an unattractive smear on the surface).

A typical laser level.

Jamb saw. This tool is designed to trim the bottom portion of door jambs to allow tiles to fit easily beneath them. The handle of the saw is positioned on top, allowing the blade of the saw to glide over the surface of the tile. It is important to remember that adding adhesive will add to the finished height of an installed tile.

Knee pads. One of the most important accessories! These are required to protect your knees during the installation process. This is one area where I would advise any reader not to skimp and save, but buy good-quality knee pads that will make a physical job less strenuous.

Laser level. Laser levels are now inexpensive tools and are easy to obtain. While not essential they can save a lot of time. However, the reader should take care to learn how to use them properly before starting work.

Margin trowel. This is a small, unnotched trowel used for applying adhesive to hard-to-reach areas. It can also be used to butter the back of tiles.

Mortar paddle. A mixing paddle will be required to mix all the setting materials.

Mortar trowel. The is the trowel used to apply the adhesive to the surface that will be receiving the stone. These trowels are available with a variety of notches and grooves that vary in width and depth. As a general guide, the smaller and lighter the stone, the shallower the notch should be. Larger, heavier, less refined stone tiles will require a trowel with deeper and bigger notches. The best rule of thumb is to use a trowel that corresponds with the depth of the tile – the larger the tile, the larger the trowel.

A typical mortar trowel. Note the notches on the sides.

A typical tape measure required for installing a stone floor.

Tape measure. It is essential to have a tape measure, which preferably should be at least 10m long.

Pencil. A pencil will be needed for marking any natural stone tiles to show where cuts should be made. It is imperative that you do not use anything other than a pencil as unsealed stone has an absorbent surface and using other implements may stain the tiles. A pencil mark is easy to remove with a damp cloth if put in the wrong place.

Plumb line/chalk line. If you are happy to get your hands dirty you may be able to make a chalk line that will do both jobs. The best products are those with a natural fibre string. Synthetic strings are to be avoided as they do not hold the chalk very well.

Rubber hammer/mallet. This is not an essential tool but can be used to tap tiles into place (without breaking them) to ensure the floor is level.

Spirit level. One of the easy ways to tell a well-laid stone floor from a badly laid one is to examine how level the floor is. Therefore, it is important to have an accurate spirit level. It would also be helpful to have a spirit level where the bubble is visible from either side so that it can be utilized in the tight corners.

A section of a floor being laid. These tiles have been fixed to the floor and have been levelled using a mallet and a spirit level.

Square edge. This is normally a straight piece of wood approximately 2m long. It is essential that it is straight and for this reason a piece of blockboard is best as it will not distort. If you are installing in a small area it may be sensible to have a short square edge as well. It is possible to buy expensive metal square edges but these are not essential and have the disadvantage that they cannot be cut down.

Water buckets. These are used to clean up any excess adhesive and grout. It is sensible to have several buckets filled with clean water located in the working area and ready for use.

PRODUCTS

There are a variety of other products you will need to source before you can lay a stone floor. The key products are listed below, but it is always worth taking the advice of the company who sold you the floor as certain natural stones do need specific additional installation products. If you follow the advice of the supplier then you will always be able to go back to the retailer should there be any problems, or if you need technical help.

Flexible Rapid-Set Adhesive

There is a vast array of different adhesives on the market at the time of writing. I would always recommend sticking to one of the major brand products such as Ardex, Dunlop, Stonefix, Weber or Bal, as they have better aftersales service should you need help. The best adhesive to purchase is a flexible one, which allows for a certain level of movement in the floor without causing the tiles to crack. If you are laying the natural stone on a floor with underfloor heating or a wooden subfloor you must always use a flexible adhesive.

I would always recommend spending a little more money and purchasing a fast-setting adhesive. This product will normally set within two hours of installation (compared with up to twenty-four hours with a standard adhesive) and this will speed up the completion of the floor. The coverage of each bag of adhesive is listed on any sales literature.

With any light-coloured stone you should use a white adhesive. With a dark stone it is preferable to use the slightly less expensive grey adhesive. If you are fixing on walls you will need to obtain a thin-bed adhesive. The stone supplier will be able to advise you on the most appropriate adhesive for your project.

A flexible, rapid-set white adhesive. There are many different brands of adhesive available and you should seek the advice of the stone retailer for the appropriate type.

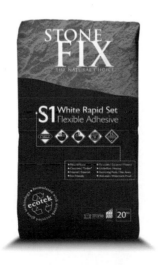

Specialist adhesives are manufactured for fixing wall tiles. This is a typical example.

A flexible rapid-set grey adhesive. This is primarily used with darker tiles and is slightly less expensive than the more common white adhesive.

Flexible Grout

As with adhesives, there is a vast array of different grouts available. Again, I would stick to one of the major branded product ranges such as Ardex, Fila, Weber, Larsens or Bal. Grouts are sold in a range of colours. Though most manufacturers tend to give their products different names, the general colours are ivory, limestone, grey and beige. If you have seen a particular floor you like in a retailer's showroom it is worth asking them what grout they have used, as a limestone grout from Ardex is not the same colour as a limestone grout from Larsens. If in any doubt it is easy to get small swatches from any reputable supplier to assist in making a decision. The basic rule of thumb is that the grout colour should match the lightest colour of the stone floor – this way you will always see the stone colour and not the grout.

The coverage of each bag of grout is listed on any sales literature. The stone supplier should also be able to advise you how many bags are required.

As with adhesives I would always recommend a flexible grout as it will allow for a certain amount of movement in the floor without cracking. You should always source a flexible grout if you are planning to use underfloor heating or are laying on a wooden subfloor.

Stone Sealer

As mentioned earlier, most sealers are impregnators. There are different brands available in the UK, but the dominant product is a sealer called Lilothin Stainstop. Different brands of sealer colour stone to different degrees and I would always recommend obtaining the sealer the retailer recommends if you want to replicate the look of the stone in their showroom. It is very important to put the right amount of sealer on the floor: if there is not enough sealer the stone will be porous, but if there is too much sealer you will be left with streaks on the natural stone floor.

The coverage of each can will be listed on the sales literature. You should also be able to get advice on how much to order from the supplier.

A flexible grout. Grout is generally available in several colours and should be matched to the lightest colour of the stone.

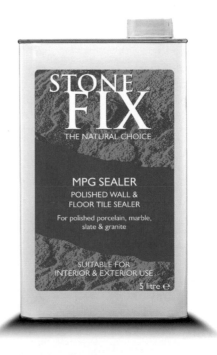

An impregnating stone sealer. There are many different brands of adhesive and you should seek the advice of the stone retailer for the appropriate type.

A roll of anti-fracture membrane.

Cleaner

Any reputable supplier will also offer a good-quality stone cleaner. These products are generally diluted with water and can easily be prepared and applied to the floor. It is important to remember that you can only use cleaners with no detergent on stone floors. Repeated use of detergent can strip of the sealer and therefore remove any protection against staining.

Wax/Finishing Products

Some natural stone floors will require finishing products to be applied to the stone after sealing has been carried out. Examples are terracotta or traditional English limestones, which will require waxing. It is worth asking the person who supplies the floor to advise if any aftercare products are required. Wax is normally applied with a buffing machine.

Anti-Fracture Membrane

This is a thin plastic membrane (approximately 4–5mm thick) designed to sit underneath the stone floor and above the subfloor. Its function is to absorb movement from the subfloor without cracking the floor above, and it will be required if you have a wooden subfloor or intend to use any

form of underfloor heating. If you have to order this product you will also need to order extra adhesive to install it.

Breathable Card Floor Protection

This is a thin layer of card that will be required to cover the floor if you have other work being carried out in the room after installation (such as fitting a kitchen). It is vital that this card is breathable to allow any moisture on the surface of the stone to escape. If you use non-breathable floor protection, moisture cannot escape from the floor, which can cause mould to grow on the floor if the protection is left down for any period of time. If installation of the floor is the last piece of work in the space this will not be required.

Self-Levelling Compound

You will need this if you are installing onto an old concrete screed and any levelling work needs to be carried out. It is applied on top of a screed to make it flat enough to lay the floor on.

Acrylic Primer

This is used to prepare a screed for the application of tiles if it is dusty or cracked.

Acrylic primer is used to prepare a screed for the application of tiles if it is dusty or cracked.

REFERENCE FORM

NAME
ADDRESS

PHONE NUMBER
MOBILE PHONE NUMBER
EMAIL ADDRESS

YEARS OF TRADING

PLEASE GIVE DETAILS BELOW OF THREE CLIENTS FOR WHOM YOU HAVE LAID A STONE FLOOR THAT YOU ARE HAPPY FOR US TO CONTACT

Client 1
Name
Address

Contact phone number
Contact mobile phone number
Type of floor you laid
Date that work was completed

Client 2
Name
Address

Contact phone number
Contact mobile phone number
Type of floor you laid
Date that work was completed

Client 3
Name
Address

Contact phone number
Contact mobile phone number
Type of floor you laid
Date that work was completed

Latex

This will be required only if you are fitting underfloor heating, as the underfloor heating mat is laid in a thin bed of latex.

FINDING A GOOD INSTALLER

If, after reading the above, you have decided you do not wish to install the floor yourself it will be necessary to find a good installer. It is wise to look at several tilers before deciding which one to use. Please also remember that this is one area where it is unlikely that the cheapest installer will do the best job. The qualities you should be seeking are a continuous track record of good and reliable work. Any competent tradesman will be happy to provide you with several references.

I would recommend checking with at least two different clients. Key areas to check up on are quality of work, timekeeping, cleanliness on site and the type of work the tiler has carried out. It does not necessarily follow that someone who normally installs a lot of travertine in bathrooms will be good at laying an antique reclaimed terracotta in a kitchen or vice versa.

In the first instance you could contact your retailer and ask them to recommend installers to you. The advantage of using their tiler will be that he will be familiar with their material and their showroom displays and will therefore know the look that you want him to replicate, although it may cost a little more.

It is important to clearly establish with your builder at which point he will prepare the floor and then to ask the installer to quote for all the work above that point. If you do this you will have a clear divide in responsibility, so if you are unfortunate enough to experience problems after installation it will be easier to identify who is responsible for the problem and therefore who should be responsible for the financial cost of putting it right.

A good installer will be able to provide you with a ballpark price in most cases without visiting the site. Once you have initial quotations it is important to ask at least two installers to visit your home and prepare a proper quote. You should clearly specify to the installer what is to be included. There are several tasks that will need to be carried out (for example, clearing rubbish, unloading the stone, disposing of the crates and so on), which you may wish the tiler to include in his quotation. Ideally you want to ensure that there are no nasty extras added to the bill at a later date.

Finally, it will be important to agree a start date with the chosen installer that allows enough time to lay the floor. Try to give him the period of time he requests and keep all other tradesman out of the room.

SITE MEASUREMENT

Before placing your final order it is really important to do a final measurement on site to ascertain the exact quantity required. It is not safe to rely on measurements from plans for several reasons:

- Plans can be inaccurate due to drawing errors.
- Plans can be inaccurate due to errors being made on site – for example, walls being built in slightly different areas from the plans.
- The scale on plans can easily be corrupted by endless photocopying and emailing.

There is nothing quite so frustrating as finding on the last day of installation that you are three tiles short or that you have ordered and paid for 5sq m of spare tiles that you do not need. While it will be possible to get more stone, this will cause delays on site and you will also incur an additional delivery charge. Therefore I strongly recommend measuring thoroughly on site and getting the quantities right.

When you have taken an accurate site measurement you should add on an extra quantity of material to cover breakage and waste on site. This extra is normally 10 per cent, but it does vary from site to site depending on the complexity of the installation. Jobs that include a large number of angles and require numerous cuts will obviously require a greater allowance for waste. If you are trying to lay a traditional hallway with tiles on a diagonal angle to the front door it may be worth raising the overage to 15 per cent.

It is also wise to store any spare tiles on site in case it should it be necessary at some point in the future to replace any stone tiles in the floor. Also, if you ever decide to extend the floor, you can give the spare tiles to the retailer to enable them to colour match the material they are currently quarrying. Remember that stone is a natural material and there is no guarantee that material extracted in three years' time will look remotely similar to material extracted today.

Floor Depth

Once you have chosen the material and confirmed the quantity you will need to tell your builder the depth of the floor and the adhesives and any other materials underneath it. The stone supplier should be able to give you this information. The builder can then ensure that the floor is prepared to the correct level, so that after the tiles are installed, they are level with the flooring finish in adjacent rooms.

DELIVERY

It is worth liaising carefully with the builder to find out when the floor will be ready for installation. If the subfloor has to be screeded, the screed will need the right amount of time to dry out. You should ask the builder for this information. Screeds that are not left for the correct time to dry can be much more susceptible to cracking and settlement, which can have severe consequences for your floor.

If the floor has had to be levelled it is also important to ensure that the self-levelling compound has dried before installing the floor.

Receiving the Delivery

Once you have placed the order the next stage in the process is to arrange the delivery date. Stone is heavy and therefore needs to be delivered on large lorries. It is important to liaise with your retailer and your builder to agree a convenient date. It is also important that you understand the delivery service the retailer is offering. Most stone is delivered by a tail-lift lorry and is a kerbside delivery.

Kerbside Delivery

This is the least expensive method of delivering stone. The lorry will reverse up to your property and will lower the tail down. The driver will have a two-wheeled pallet truck to move the crates of stone around. This delivery can be problematic if your property is on a hill, if there are any overhanging trees or if you have a gravel drive. Generally a tail-lift lorry can deliver stone to anywhere that a skip can be delivered. If you have a gravel drive you must ask your builder to leave some sheets of plywood at the property. The driver will then unload the crates onto the plywood and this will prevent his pallet truck sinking into the gravel. If in any doubt you should talk to the person organizing the delivery to resolve any concerns before the delivery date.

A kerbside delivery will not include unloading the stone or moving it into your property. Therefore if you need to bring the stone into the property on the day of delivery you must arrange to be on site (or ask the builder to do this) to receive the delivery and bring it into the property. If you live in a city and have no drive, a kerbside delivery will be left on the roadside and therefore must be unloaded straight after delivery, so you may need to arrange extra labour to be present to help unload the stone.

Crane Arm Delivery

If a kerbside delivery cannot be carried out at your property you will almost certainly need a crane arm delivery, which is a much more flexible form of delivery. The lorry will be equipped with a crane arm and therefore can lift the stone over fences, hedges and so on, and onto grass if need be. However, this is more expensive than a kerbside delivery.

Checking the Delivery

When the stone is delivered it is obviously important to check that it has arrived in good condition. The following things should be checked while the driver is unloading:

- Check the delivery note to ensure all items are present and are as ordered.
- Check that the crates appear to be structurally whole and show no signs of being bent, cracked or out of shape.
- Check that the polythene wrapping on top of the crates is intact.

If you are in any doubt on any of the above you should sign the delivery note with the details of your concern and report it to the person who sold you the stone. It is also worth taking a Stanley knife and opening the top of each crate. Things to check are that the corners on tiles look intact and that there is no obvious breakage. If a small number of tiles have cracked or damaged corners this is nothing to be concerned about – remember that you have added 10 per cent to your order quantity to allow for cut tiles near walls and simply allocate these tiles straight into these areas.

Any fixing products, such as adhesive, grout and sealer, must be carried into the house as soon as they are delivered. If adhesive or grout get wet it can cause them to set, making them completely unusable.

Checking the Colour

As mentioned earlier, stone is cut from block to tile with a diamond-tipped saw. This has water fired at it to keep it cool. A consequence of this is that if the stone is loaded quickly from the production line into a crate it can be wet when it arrives on site. Some stones change colour significantly when they are wet and revert to their normal colour when dry.

When you open up the crate it is worth taking four tiles from across the delivery from the crate immediately and moving them inside the property. These tiles should be put somewhere warm (such as a boiler cupboard or against a radiator) to dry them out. Most stone should be completely dry within a day of being stored in this way. These tiles will then act as your control before installation starts and will be important throughout the process. As the stone starts to dry you will notice it gets lighter at the corners first. This is perfectly normal. When it is completely dry it should be slightly lighter than the retailer's display floor or any sealed samples you have been given.

If there are any exceptional tiles with very strong colour or fossil this is not a cause for concern. You are dealing with a natural material that will contain variations. These tiles can also be used for the cuttings and clippings.

If you have any concerns over the colour after taking these steps they should be reported to the person who sold you the stone.

Unloading the Stone

It is now time to unload the stone and bring it into the property. The stone should ideally be moved to one end of the room (or very near to it) where

This picture shows the difference between wet and dry stone. These tiles are identical in colour when dry. The tile on the left was run under a tap and you can clearly see how the colour has changed. This shows how important it is that the stone is dry before you start installation.

1. Concrete screed with no underfloor heating.

wall

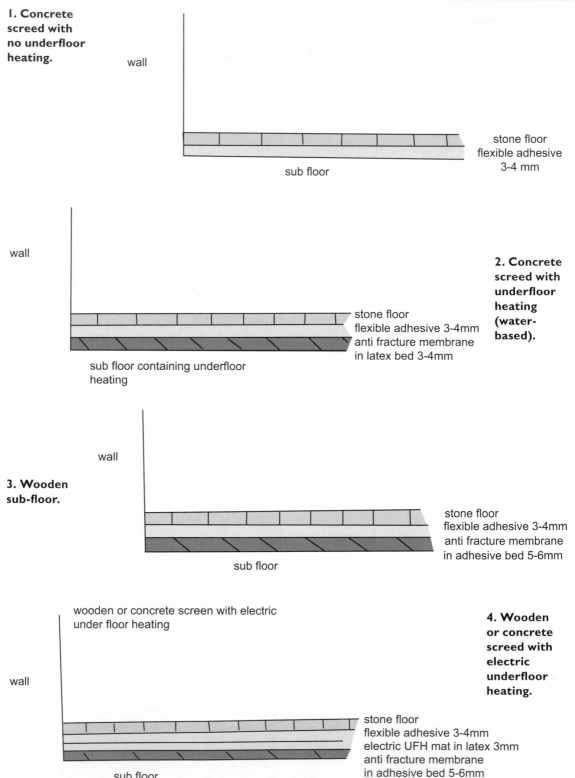

stone floor
flexible adhesive
3-4 mm

sub floor

wall

2. Concrete screed with underfloor heating (water-based).

stone floor
flexible adhesive 3-4mm
anti fracture membrane
in latex bed 3-4mm

sub floor containing underfloor heating

wall

3. Wooden sub-floor.

stone floor
flexible adhesive 3-4mm
anti fracture membrane
in adhesive bed 5-6mm

sub floor

wooden or concrete screen with electric under floor heating

4. Wooden or concrete screed with electric underfloor heating.

wall

stone floor
flexible adhesive 3-4mm
electric UFH mat in latex 3mm
anti fracture membrane
in adhesive bed 5-6mm

sub floor

work will be carried out. It should be stacked up against the wall in piles, with a small gap at the bottom of each tile so air can get to both faces of the tile.

This will help the tiles to dry out. It is better if the room is dry and well ventilated. If you have wet plaster on the walls it is important to keep all windows and doors open during the day and you may wish to consider bringing in a dehumidifier to speed up the drying out process further.

As you unload the stone it is worth pulling out any tiles with colour and variation you are less keen on and putting them in a pile for cuttings and clips. If there are tiles with fossils or colours you wish to make a feature of, it is again worth separating these tiles so that they can be laid in heavy traffic areas where they can be seen.

PREPARATION OF THE SUBFLOOR

The next stage is the preparation of the subfloor to allow for installation. Any stone floor needs a good firm hard and level base. The most common types of subfloor are listed below.

Concrete Screed

This is the best subfloor for a stone floor as it provides a firm, hard base with little risk of movement. Any old screed should be carefully examined for signs of movement or cracking. It should also be checked to ensure it is level. This is best done with a careful visual inspection and a laser level. To correct any level deficiencies you need to apply some self-levelling compound to the affected area to. Once this has had time to set you are ready to lay your floor.

If you are putting a floor down in a new extension it is likely that you will be dealing with a new concrete screed, which will be sourced and laid by your builder. The key issue with a new screed is asking the builder how thick it will be and to specify when it will be ready to lay a floor. Building standards state that you should wait six weeks before installation starts. Leaving the appropriate time for the screed to dry is vitally import-ant, as any new screed will settle as it dries and contracts. It is obviously important at this stage to do everything possible to speed

How to stack up the stone when it is unloaded from the crate. The tiles have been stacked with air gaps between each tile to ensure the stone can dry out.

up the drying-out, such as ensuring the space is well ventilated and possibly hiring a dehumidifier. Laying the floor on the screed before it has fully dried out can risk movement in the screed and lead to cracking in the floor.

It is possible to lay stone on a wet screed by using an anti-fracture membrane. If you decide to go down this route you can lay a floor as soon as the screed is firm enough to walk on (generally one to two weeks). If you wish to try this, check with the anti-fracture membrane supplier at which point they believe their product can be laid on a wet screed.

Wooden Floors

Natural stone can be laid on solid or suspended wooden floors but it is important to do the necessary preparation.

First, you have to make a judgement on the quality of the wooden flooring. If the floor is in good condition it should only be necessary to fit either dukka board (an insulation board) or anti-fracture membrane onto the floorboards and then lay the natural stone on top.

If the wooden floor is in a poor condition the best approach is to lift the floorboards and fit sheets of plywood across the joists. These should be screwed down securely. The anti-fracture membrane should then be applied on top of the plywood and the stone then fitted on top of this.

It is very important with any wooden subfloor that you fit either an anti-fracture membrane or dukka board to allow for the movement that occurs in every wooden floor. If you do not do this you run a significant risk that over time cracks will develop in the tiles caused by movement underneath.

UNDERFLOOR HEATING

Over the last ten years there has been significant growth in the number of buildings where underfloor heating is being installed. Natural stone is a perfect complement to underfloor heating as it is a conductor. If you wish to see how effectively it transmits heat, put a small stone sample on a radiator and leave it for ten minutes. When you come back you will find the heat has transmitted through the stone effectively.

There are currently two major types of underfloor heating laid in the UK.

Water-Based Underfloor Heating

This is a system of pipes that are laid in the screed and are connected to the central heating system. As they are pipes they add about 6cm to the floor height and therefore this system is more common in new houses. As the pipes are in the screed, installation would need to be carried out by the builder. When you turn on a pipe-based

A typical electric underfloor heating mat after installation.

The electric underfloor heating mat with a layer of latex spread over a section of it.

underfloor heating system it will expand slightly and when you turn it off it will contract, so you are introducing a little bit of movement into a solid floor. To protect the floor from this movement, you must use an anti-fracture membrane and flexible adhesive and grout.

Electric Underfloor Heating Mats

There is a vast array of different mats sold for use as underfloor heating. These are laid on top of the screed in a bed of latex and the wire is pulled through the stone floor to be controlled by a thermostat, which is usually fitted to a wall near the floor. As this method only adds approximately 6mm to the floor height this is the most common system of underfloor heating in any property where a room is being extended or simply having the floor changed (as it will not put the floor levels that far away from any adjoining rooms).

There are many different specifications of matting, ranging from back-up systems to supplement radiators to single-source floor mats. If you take a plan of the room to an underfloor heating specialist he will be able to calculate the heat loss from the room and specify the perfect system for your property.

As the matting is laid on top of the screed it is normally installed with the floor. This is a fairly straightforward process and there is no reason, if you are laying your own floor, that you should not attempt this. It is done in the following stages:

1. Lay a thin bed of latex on the subfloor (normally 2mm thick).
2. Lay the sheets of matting in the latex, making sure you manipulate them to get into all the necessary corners of the room. It is obviously not necessary to lay the matting in any area where furniture will be placed.

ABOVE: **The heating mat with a layer of latex spread over it.**

BELOW: **The completed room ready for installation. The latex needs to be dry prior to tiling.**

The finished subfloor with the wet latex drying on top.

3. When the latex has set test the matting.
4. Pull the wire for the thermostat through to the place where the thermostat will be located.
5. Lay another thin bed of latex on top of the matting and wait for it to dry.
6. Test the floor mat again before installing any flooring on top.

Whether you choose a water-based system or electric mat system, it is important to ensure that you follow rigorously the instructions for warming up the heating when the floor is finished. The screed will still be settling and therefore sudden changes in temperature can cause it to crack or sag. If this happens it can cause sections of the floor above to sag or crack as well.

It is also essential, with any form of underfloor heating, that you use an anti-fracture membrane as well as flexible adhesives and grouts between the subfloor and the stone to allow for the additional movement this will cause.

INSTALLATION OF THE FLOOR

At this point you should now be in a position where:

1. You have bought or borrowed all the tools needed.
2. The stone has been delivered to your property and has been bought inside.

3. The control tiles have been dried out and separated from the main batch.
4. The ancillary products have been sourced and are on site.
5. Any subfloor preparation has been carried out.
6. Any underfloor heating has been installed.

If all this has been done, you are ready to begin the process of installing the floor.

Stage 1 – Preparation

Concrete Screed
If you are installing on a concrete slab the first stage is to ensure that the stone will bond to the screed. First, you should clean the screed to ensure that it is free of any excess dirt, paint or other building products, and apply acrylic primer if necessary. You should check the screed for any high spots. This can be done with a level or a long piece of rigid metal. Do not use a piece of timber for this task as it may be bent or twisted and give you a misleading impression of how level the floor is. A chalk line or laser level can also be used as a very simple method of checking the consistency within the slab.

You should begin by snapping lines from various different corners of the room to give you different angles across the floor. You should then observe where the chalk line is lightest or non existent. This indicates the location of the high spots and these should be marked on the slab.

Identifying the high spots is very important as when you have identified these you will be able to ascertain the height at which the floor will meet any floors in the next rooms. It is rare that you will encounter a floor that is perfectly flat and you should expect to find some variations.

A laser level is a vital tool for checking the subfloor is level.

If the variations are significant it is important to deal with them before installing the floor. It is possible to fill low spots with adhesive, but the best solution is to use a self-levelling compound. Once this has been mixed it will flow naturally into the lower areas, creating a flat, level surface.

You should check the area again once the self-levelling compound has set. It is important to identify the highest area in the floor so that you can start the installation from this point. Any lower spots in the floor can be dealt with by building up the adhesive bed to level them up.

You should also inspect the screed for any cracks and ensure that an anti-fracture membrane is specified to be fitted over any cracks. This membrane is designed to expand with any cracks or movement in the floor without fracturing or cracking the tile above. If you are using any kind of underfloor heating (water-based or electric matting) you should use an anti-fracture membrane as well as flexible adhesives and grouts.

Wooden Subfloor

If you are installing on a wooden subfloor, the first task is to study the quality of the floor. Remember that stone requires a good, firm, hard and true base. If the floorboards are in good condition the next step is to clean them and remove any dirt or building residue on the top surface.

If the condition of the wooden floorboards is less good you then need to determine the best way of providing a flat, level, hard base. This may be by changing a couple of boards or by removing the floor boards and stripping the floor back to the joists.

If you decide to remove the boards it will be necessary to obtain some sheets of plywood and screw them to the joists. These should be mounted securely to the joists at 300mm centres.

Whichever of the two routes you follow, you will still have a floor that has an element of movement and flexibility, which will only be increased if you decide to add underfloor heating. It is essential with any wooden floor, therefore, to add a product to deal with this flexibility. There are two choices, but whichever option you choose, it is essential that you use flexible adhesives and grouts.

Anti-fracture membrane. This is the best product to use if you have a solid floor underneath the floor boards, or if there is no underfloor heating, as it is thinner than the other alternative (an insulation board). This is a thin plastic membrane that is laid in a thin bed of latex on the subfloor. This is clearly the best option if you are trying to keep floor height down. The anti-fracture membrane should be cleaned once installed and all dust and dirt removed so that the stone can bond properly onto the membrane.

Insulation board (dukka board). This is a flexible board designed to insulate the space above. If you are fitting a stone floor on a suspended floor (for example, above an open cellar) this is a better option than an anti-fracture membrane as it will stop heat escaping from the room above into the cellar. It is also worth considering the use of insulation board in any situation with underfloor heating for the same reasons – it will maximize the effect of the underfloor heating. The board is fixed onto the subfloor with adhesive. It should then be cleaned thoroughly to give a good bond between it and the stone.

Shower or Wet Room Floors

Installation of a shower or wet room floor is more complex than any other floor and it is important to take great care. You must identify the position of the drain and build up the subfloor to allow installation of the tiles with a fall towards the drain to allow for proper drainage and ensure that no standing water is left on the stone. It is also necessary to fit a damp-proof membrane under the tiles to ensure that if any water does leak through a joint it cannot damage the subfloor.

Any shower wall should be clad on all sides with cement board. This should be screwed directly into the stud walls and must include any niches. This is to ensure that if any moisture gets behind the tiles it has nowhere to go and cannot damage the walls.

Stage 2 – Installation

Understanding your Material

It is vitally important to remember that your floor is a natural material and will contain variation. A

The material in this photo has a wide variety of colours and sizes, and it is vital to ensure that these are spread across the floor evenly. You can only do this by examining the stone carefully after it is unloaded from the crate before installing it.

good professional installer will go through every delivery so that he has a good understanding of the colour variation. It is essential to go through your order and divide the stone by colour and variation. If there are any tiles that contain strong markings or variations they should be put to one side at this stage. Tiles with markings that you like can be placed in the middle of the floor where they can be seen; those you are less keen on can be used for cuts and clips or laid where furniture will be placed on top of them.

Antique reclaimed stone, antique reclaimed terracotta, slate and some sandstones are all materials that contain some variations in depth, so again it is a good idea to go through the stone delivery and group it into various thicknesses. You should begin the installation with the thickest

tiles and complete it using the thinnest tiles. If you work in this order you can build up the thinnest tiles with additional adhesive and it will be much easier to create a level, flat floor.

Identifying Where to Start

A key point in laying a floor is deciding where to start the installation. If this is done properly it will make the installation much easier to complete. It will also identify any difficult sections of the room so adjustments can be planned to eliminate these areas.

The first thing to do is to identify the centre line of the space. This is not intended to mark the position of the joint; it is a base for measurement and nothing more. The centre line will only be a true central line in a perfectly rectangular room, where it is simply a matter of finding the middle point of the two shortest walls. If there is a particular wall that you wish the floor to be parallel to, you should make the points in the middle, ensuring that they are equidistant from the wall.

The marks are joined together by stretching a chalk line between the marks. You then lift it from the floor, staying as close to the middle line as possible, and then let it fall back onto the floor to create a clean and straight line.

The next point is to identify the cross line. This must be exactly at right angles to the base line. It is not wise to use a wall for this measurement in case there are subtle curves to the wall. It is safer to use a large set square or laser level set to 90 degrees.

You should then dry fit the tiles to check that all the measurements are correct and that tiles of equal size line up around the perimeter of the room. The first thing a neutral eye will spot about a badly laid floor is thin cuts of stone against a wall. This is to be avoided at all costs. It is vitally important to ensure the first row of tiles is straight. Any error here will be replicated across the floor. Laying out the tiles in a dry fit gives you the opportunity to make any changes in terms of the colour of size mix. When you are happy it is important to stack the tiles in the order that you wish to lay them.

Laying the Floor

Now that you have dry laid the tiles and understand the material it is time actually to start laying the floor.

The first stage is preparing the fixing materials, and the first product to use is the tiling adhesive.

Overcoming level differences between two floors. In this example a piece of slate was chamfered and fitted on an angle to ensure a flat, trip-free join between the two floors. This is known as a threshold piece.

TOP: **Here you can see an example of a wooden threshold to join together two floors that are very different in appearance.**

BELOW: **A random pattern floor being installed. The floor laying pattern can be seen for guidance. The tiles have been laid out dry (without adhesive) so the installer can work out the grout spacing. You can see the blue tile spacer on top of a tile.**

There is a variety of different tile adhesives and it is important to specify the correct product. For most floors you should use a thick-bed, flexible, rapid-set stone adhesive. The adhesive must be thick-bed so you can build up the floor if needed to overcome any variation in the screed. The adhesive must be rapid-set and flexible for the reasons raised earlier in the section on under-floor heating. For most wall tiles you should use a flexible wall adhesive, and again, a rapid-set adhesive will set quicker and will allow faster installation.

It is vitally important to prepare the adhesive properly. It needs to be consistent and firm enough so that the trowel ridges do not collapse under the weight of the tile. If the adhesive is too wet the tiles will sink and this will lead to an uneven floor. If the adhesive is too dry it may not adhere to the back of the stone or the screed, which will cause it to debond at a later date.

It is also important to use a white adhesive for light-coloured stones and a grey adhesive for darker stones.

The adhesive should be applied to the back of the tile in much the same way that you would spread butter on bread. It is important that as much of the tile is covered as possible to ensure a better bond between the screed and the tile. It is very simple to back butter a tile. Apply a thin layer of adhesive using the unnotched edge of the trowel.

Then it is important to check the levels on the floor. When setting each tile you should gently press the corners of each tile and use your finger-tips to level it with the tile next to it. Keep your level nearby so that you can check as you go along. It is much easier to adjust the levels when the tile has just been installed.

It is normal to have to adjust and lift a couple of tiles to get the floor level and this is nothing to be concerned about.

How to apply adhesive to the back of the tile. It should be applied evenly.

ABOVE: **Levelling the floor. The tiles have been fixed to the floor and are being levelled with the aid of a spirit level. This is done by tapping the top of the tiles while the adhesive is soft.**

RIGHT: **Levelling a Roman opus floor during installation using the appropriate levels.**

A simple brass or silver case can hide a power point and avoid it being an eyesore.

TOP: **With a traditional flagstone, the grout line should be set wider to give a more rustic look. The large random-length tiles also enhance the rustic look.**

BELOW: **A modern grey honed marble. In this example the grout line has been set as tight as possible to get the crispest look possible.**

When you are satisfied that the tile is level you should wipe away any surplus adhesive from the surface of each tile. Do not allow this adhesive to set on the tile as it can be very difficult to remove once dry. The adhesive should be allowed to set for at least twenty-four hours and it is important to ensure newly laid tiles are clearly marked and that no one walks on them. It is a wise idea to put a temporary barrier around the area where the tiles have been laid to ensure that no one can walk on it.

It is also important to ensure you have set your grout joints to the correct size. This is easy to do and if in doubt you should use tile spacers to ensure the gaps are consistent.

This is especially relevant if you are fixing up a wall where any variation will be obvious. It is customary to use tighter grout joints with modern, more contemporary floors and slightly wider grout joints with aged floors.

A wide variety of floors are sold in repeat random patterns, and many of these are not prepared to give an exact grout joint. Therefore, when you lay out the pattern, it is very important to manipulate the tiles by hand to make sure that the pattern works and can be repeated on the floor. If you wish to lay a particular pattern, it

An aged limestone floor. Due to the nature of the repeat pattern the tile sizes will vary slightly. Therefore it is important for the installer to line the pattern up, manually adjusting the grout joints to minimize this effect.

If you are fitting a riven stone it is important to skim the surface of the tile to fill in any large fossil holes with grout prior to sealing. Here the grout is the slightly lighter patches in the surface of the tile. After that, apply a protective liquid, such as Multiseal, to stop dirt from being ground into the surface.

is a good idea to visit the retailer, look carefully at the display and measure the grout joints. It would be unusual for any random repeat pattern to have the same grout joint across the floor, but as these patterns are normally used for more rustic floors it is not such an important point.

Sealer – First Coat

Once you have laid the tiles it is important to ensure the floor is given adequate time to dry out. Some stone will be wet when delivered to site and it is important to ensure it is dry before you go any further. Earlier on I suggested that when the stone is delivered it is worth taking out two tiles from the crate and drying them out. These controls will now be very useful, as you can use

them to compare to the laid floor to be certain it is dry.

Once it is dry, it is time to seal the floor with the appropriate impregnating sealer. The selection of the appropriate sealer was discussed above. It is very important that any dust or dirt is removed from the stone before applying the first coat of sealer, because otherwise the dirt will be sealed into the floor. The easiest way to do this is to wash the face of the stone with a damp cloth.

The sealer should be spread evenly across the surface of the tiles with a spray gun, sponge, mop or brush. If you see any white streaks forming as the sealer dries, wipe them off. These marks are caused by excess sealer on the stone and will make the stone become streaky if they are not

A tiler in the process of sealing the floor. You can see how the stone has changed colour in the area where the sealant has just been applied. Stone Classics

removed. The stone will absorb the sealer, which is what it is supposed to do. The first coat of sealer is very important as it protects the stone from staining during the installation process and makes cleaning up after grouting much easier. At all times it is important to follow the manufacturer's instructions. As long as the sealing is done correctly the stone will be a low maintenance and practical floor. Again, it is important that no one walks on the floor while the sealer is drying.

Grout

The next stage is to grout the floor. The selection of the appropriate grout and the grout colour were discussed above. If you are in any doubt about the grout colour, make up some samples of the shortlisted colours and try them in the room against the chosen stone.

The grout should be mixed to the consistency of cake icing and should be applied using a grout trowel on a wet sponged tile. It is important to remove any excess grout from the tile surface as you go along, and to check the surface of the stone as the material dries for any haze left by the grout. It is much easier to remove this when the grout is wet rather than after it has dried out. A practical tip is to keep plenty of buckets of clean and clear water nearby so they are ready to hand for this purpose. Another practical tip is to have a grout-filled sponge in one bucket and a bucket of water next to it for speedy rinsing.

The best approach is to clean the tile with a damp sponge: making only one pass over the tile and then turn the sponge over to make a second pass. After this rinse the sponge. Do not use a sponge that is too wet as it may create efflorescence or discolour the grout. After application you should leave the grout to dry out according to the manufacturer's instructions.

Sealer – Second and Third Coats

When you are certain the grout is dry, wash the surface of the floor again to remove any dust or dirt and again wait for the floor to dry. Then apply a second and a third coat of the impregnating sealer, leaving each coat to fully dry before going any further. You will find that the stone will absorb less sealer on the second coat and still less when the third coat is put down. This is to be expected. It is very important at this stage to ensure that no excess sealer is left on the surface of the stone

but is wiped off as it appears. This can be done using a buffing machine.

A more porous stone will absorb more sealer. However, it is important even with a very hard stone to ensure that the third coat is applied. There is a simple test to ascertain whether you have enough sealer on the stone. Take a glass of water and pour a small amount in several places across the floor. Leave it for sixty seconds, then take up the water with an absorbent cloth or paper towel. If the sealer has been applied properly the water will pool on the surface and will come away without leaving any water mark on the floor. If it does leave a water mark, more sealer is required. It is quite normal for there to be sufficient sealer in one area but to require more in another.

The tiler has grouted this section of the floor and is now wiping the surface of the tiles clean to remove grout residue. Stone Classics

The recently sealed floor is being buffed with a buffing machine to spread the sealer evenly across the floor.

This is because you are dealing with a natural material and the density will vary slightly across the floor. As it is imperative that the whole floor is sealed correctly, it is really worth taking time over this: the vast majority of problems with stone floors are caused by the sealing not being done correctly.

Final Treatments

When you are certain the floor is sealed correctly and has dried out properly, you can apply any final treatments. If you are having a traditional floor you may choose to wax the floor to enhance the fossil and colour of the floor. Wax is normally applied with a buffing machine.

Other liquids can also be applied; it is best to consult the retailer on the most appropriate product for your floor.

If you have chosen an open-grained material, such as a terracotta or a limestone with a textured surface, it is important to think about putting a protective coat on top of the floor to stop dirt getting ground into the stone. The best product on the market in the UK at the time of writing is a Lilothin product called Multiseal. This is transparent so does not change the colour of the stone.

A traditional floor immediately after wax has been applied to it. You can clearly see the additional sheen on the tiles.

INSTALLING MOSAIC

Mosaic is supplied in sheets, which are normally 30cm × 30cm. It is installed in a similar way to tiles.

1. Remove the paper from the back of the mosaic mesh and carefully check each mesh for any loose or damaged tiles. Then apply the adhesive to the area where the mosaic will be fixed, whether it is the wall or the floor. Butter the adhesive as described above for tiles.
2. Apply the mosaic mesh to the adhesive, tapping it with a wooden block or a wooden mallet to ensure it is level. It is also useful to use a spirit level to ensure that each piece of mosaic is level with the next and/or the tiles next to it.
3. Allow the adhesive to dry out (twenty-four hours should normally suffice), then apply the grout to the mosaic with a trowel, as described above for tiles. The grout should be carefully selected to match the lightest tile colour in the mosaic. You must be careful to ensure that any grout that left on the top of the mosaic is removed while it is wet.
4. Once the grout is dry, apply a stone sealer to the mosaic. Each sheet of mosaic should be sealed at least three times to ensure it is properly protected. The process of sealing will raise any fossil and colour details in the stone.

The mosaic should be treated exactly as a stone tile in terms of care and maintenance – that is, treated with a stone cleaner and resealed every four to five years. It also means not using any detergent-based cleaners on the mosaic.

A common issue with stone flooring – tiles that have 'picture framed' to the edges. This is caused by water moisture and is solved by using a liquid such as Wexa to break down the mark and then leaving it to dry.

TROUBLESHOOTING

There are a number of common issues that can go wrong with stone flooring that are caused by installation mistakes and can easily be resolved once identified.

Picture framing. This is where the stone tile get darker all the way round the edge but remains the true colour in the middle of the tile. This is caused by water from the grout entering the edge of tile and not escaping. The easiest way to resolve this is to scrub the edges of the tile with an aggressive cleaner such as Wexa.

Smearing to the stone surface. This can often be seen when light shines across the surface of a newly laid floor. It is caused by too much sealer

This photo shows a possible problem with stone after sealing. The white residue on top of the stone needs to be removed or it will cause smears.

being applied to the floor and not being wiped away, and can be dealt with by scrubbing the surface of the tiles with an abrasive cleaner such as Wexa. The surface of the stone should then be washed with water.

Darker patches in the middle of the tiles. This is caused by the floor not being left for enough time before sealing, and the darker patches are where the water is concentrated. If only a few tiles are affected, it should be left as it will dissipate over time. If it is more widespread than this the sealer needs to be stripped off the floor again and the floor left until it is dry.

Grout smears on the stone surface. If this occurs you should purchase a specialist product designed to break up the grout residue and remove it.

Grout breaking up. If the grout is loose and starts flaking away it should be chiselled out and replaced.

Salt/white deposits coming through the floor. This can sometimes occur when water deposits come through the stone as salt. They should be wiped away as they appear. This problem should cease in the first few weeks after the floor has been finished.

The floor collecting dirt. This may be indicative of the sealer not working effectively, therefore it is imperative to test it. This can be done by taking a glass of water and pouring it onto the floor in five or six different places. Leave the floor for about sixty seconds and then try to lift the water with an absorbent material such as a paper towel or a cloth. If the water comes up without leaving a mark on the floor the sealer is working correctly, and the floor needs to be cleaned thoroughly and the cause of the dirt identified. If the sealer is faulty, however, the floor needs to be resealed.

Dirt streaks appearing on the floor. If you notice streaks of dirt appearing on the floor (rather than general dirt as described above) this is normally an indicator that the wrong cleaner (one containing detergent) is being used. The streaks are where the tassels on the mop (laden with detergent) have stripped the sealer and dirt has got in. The floor should be cleaned thoroughly and resealed.

Tiles start cracking. This is normally caused by movement underneath the floor, most commonly by screed settlement. If screed movement occurs it normally cracks floors in doorways or where screeds meet. Screed movement has usually stopped within six to nine months of the floor being fitted. It is best to leave the cracks until you are certain they are not getting any bigger and then replace the affected tiles. If you wait until the cracks are not growing you can be confident that any underfloor movement has stopped.

Another potential issue with stone flooring. The shadow in some parts of the grout line shows where the grout has not been finished flush to the stone. This is easy to resolve but it is obviously important to match the grout colour exactly.

CHAPTER 6

Installing Kitchen Fittings

TOOLS

The following tools will be needed for an easy installation:

- Tape measure
- Stanley knife
- Spirit level
- Pencil
- Masking tape
- Drill
- Screws and rawl plugs
- Wooden battens to provide support on the walls for the worktops where necessary
- Packers and shims so you can level the worktops effectively
- Epoxy glue resin.

Obviously you will also need the relevant safety equipment:

- Safety glasses
- Safety lifting belt
- Safety boots
- Disposable gloves.

If a sink is to be fitted in the worktop you will also need a hygienic clear silicone for gluing and securing the sink.

You will also require a stone sealer as well as a stone cleaner for ongoing maintenance.

PRE-INSTALLATION

A large natural stone worktop will be very heavy. It is essential that you have enough manpower on hand to lift the top safely. This will include bringing it in from the delivery vehicle and lifting it into place.

It is also important to make sure that enough supports are in place to hold up the top when it is placed over the furniture. Where the worktops sit over kitchen appliances and carcass units, or where they go into corners of the room, you must fit wooden battens to the walls to support the worktop.

INSTALLATION

If you are working in a kitchen it is sensible to remove any cupboard door fronts during the fitting of the tops. It is also sensible to trial fit the worktops prior to installation. Bring the worktops into the room and place them on the furniture. If you wish you can then trial fit the sink or hob to ensure there is enough space. If there is

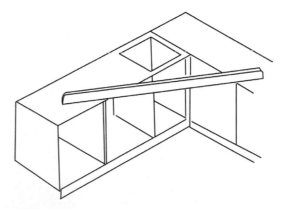

Using a long spirit level to ensure base cupboards are level before putting the granite worktop on top.

It is important that templates also show the position of tap holes. Note the granite drainer grooves.

not, you will have to cut away part of the base unit to allow space for the taps and the sink or hob. You should always allow an additional 5–15mm for movement. Do not forget to allow for all the pipe work either. Once any unwanted material has been removed you can then refit the pieces and check this again.

When you fit the tops it is then necessary to ensure they are level. This can be done with a long spirit level. If there are any corners, remember to place the spirit level across the corner to ensure all is level.

It is normal that adjustments will need to be made. This can be done with plastic packers or shims to level the tops. You can also adjust the plastic legs of the base units to alter the levels. You should also ensure all joints are flush and consistent. There are other methods to ensure

tops are level, such as rolling a round coin over the tops: if it rolls in a straight line, the top is level.

After you have checked the levels, check that all overhangs are consistent and an equal distance from front of the piece of furniture underneath.

FITTING THE SINK

Any taps should be fitted prior to installation of the sink. When the natural stone top is fitted, you should ensure that you have cleaned the edge of the worktop where the sink is to meet it. This is important to ensure the glue can adhere properly to the surface of the stone.

Silicone should be applied to the sink and the granite so that they fix together properly. It is sometimes helpful to put water in the sink to weigh it down. You must ensure that any excess

In this photo you can see a kitchen worktop made from a nero tuscana honed granite top. Note the full-size granite upstands.

silicone is removed with a damp cloth before it sets and dries.

If you are fitting an under-mounted sink, the dimensions for the hole in the granite must be 10–20mm less than the dimensions of the sink. This will ensure a good fit between the sink and the top. Most under-mounted sinks have a set of bolts and fittings supplied with them. The normal process of installation is as follows. First, clean the worktop and the sink carefully where the glue is to be applied. After this you should apply masking tape to the sink cut, then silicone to the sink edge and the worktop bottom where the cutout is located.

You should mount the sink from the inside of the carcass and then fit and tighten the screw bolts evenly. After this apply a thin bead of silicone between the sink and the cutout. Remove any excess silicone with a damp cloth and then finally remove the masking tape.

If you are installing a hob you should stick a foam seal around the hob to ensure nothing gets between the worktop and hob.

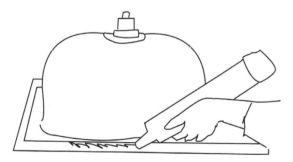

Applying silicone to the case of the skink before applying the sink to the base cupboards. After the sink is fixed, the granite is fixed on top and the joint between the sink and the top should be siliconed together.

Here you can see how the underslung sink has been fitted into the worktop. It is imperative in this situation to template the top and to ensure the measurement and position of the sink is accurate.

GLUING STONE JOINTS

When you come to this part of the task you will need disposal gloves, more masking tape and a Stanley knife.

The first step is to mark the worktop edges with masking tape on each side of the joint. You must remember to mask the front edges.

When the worktops are in place it is time to

In this installation the base cupboards and then the sink have been fitted, then the granite worktop with the upstand. The furniture installer will then return to the site to fit the tongue and groove and taps.

How to deal with granite upstands round the back of a cooker and the legs of a chimney. The upstand is half the size around the chimney leg in order to stop it becoming a dominant feature.

glue the joints. The joints should be glued with either a silicone or a two-part epoxy glue. You should take care to select a colour that matches the colour of the stone that you have chosen. If you decide to use an epoxy glue you may need to add a colour pigment to the epoxy before applying the hardener so that the worktop and the joints blend into the natural stone. When you glue the tops you should apply a very fine line of glue on the joint where the worktop pieces meet (or where the worktop meets the wall).

After the glue has dried you should remove the masking tape. It is normal for epoxy or silicone to dry in 5–10 minutes. If you find any excess dry glue or silicone on the worktop this should be removed carefully with a sharp Stanley knife, taking care not to scratch the stone.

After the tops have been fixed together you should then glue the worktops to the base furniture by using clear silicone. Run the silicone around all the edges where the base furniture and the supports meet the natural stone. It is important to reach all the places possible. Again, it is important to remove any excess silicone or glue with a damp cloth.

INSTALLATION OF SPLASHBACK, UPSTANDS AND WINDOWSILLS

These are fitted in a very similar way to the worktops. It is worth noting that in the vast majority of properties the walls are rarely straight or square so small gaps between worktops and the walls are to be expected. Rather than altering the work-tops, it may actually be more practical to alter the walls to minimize the gaps. It is therefore most sensible to fit the splashbacks and upstands after the worktop is fitted.

First, trial fit the pieces on top of the worktop, checking the size as well as the colour match with the main worktop. If any adjustments are needed these can be processed on site.

To install, apply silicone on the rear side of the piece of stone, then press and hold it in place.

When the silicone has set, apply a clear sili-cone to the edge between the worktop and the upstand. This is very important to ensure this joint is completely watertight.

After installation you must seal the join between the walls and the worktop with low modulus silicone. After this the worktops, upstands and so on must be cleaned very carefully, then sealed three times with an impregnating sealer. You must wait for each coat of sealer to dry, and take care to wipe away any sealer residue. If you do not do this it will cause smears to appear on the stone.

Windowsills are fitted in exactly the same way as a splashback. The edge detail to the front of the sill should ideally match another edge details/ architectural detail

CARE AND MAINTENANCE

The care and maintenance of worktops, upstands, sills or any other stone items is exactly the same as for a natural stone floor. You must never use detergent-based cleaners as over time they will strip the sealer from the stone. There is a variety of non-detergent based cleaners widely available from most good DIY stores or large supermar-kets. Please also bear in mind that the tops will need resealing every four to five years.

CHAPTER 7

Installing a Fireplace

Limestone and marble fireplaces are easy to measure and install for anyone who is competent at DIY. This is best carried out in several easy steps.

MEASURING YOUR SPACE

First, measure the depth, height and width of the opening. Pass these measurements on to the retailer who is supplying the fireplace. At this time it is also important to decide how you wish to finish the inside of the fireplace. If you are planning to paint the inside of the opening you can give the retailer the exact dimensions. If you are planning to fit a stone, cast iron or vermiculite lining you must deduct the thickness of the lining from the width. This is very important as you want the inside of the hearth will line up correctly with the lining.

If you are installing a new hearth it is also important to deduct the height of the hearth from the height of the opening to ensure the mantle fits correctly to the opening height.

If the opening is smaller than the inside of the fireplace the retailer will supply you with a set of slips. These are rectangular pieces of stone that fit inside the fireplace and finish flush with the inside of the lining.

INSTALLATION

Once the fireplace has been manufactured the process of installation is quite simple. Unload the fireplace, taking care to check all the pieces for cracks and marks.

Check the floor and walls to ensure they are level and remove any skirting boards. If the floor is not level you must look for any high spots and use the high spots as the level. You will have to build up the sand and cement in the other areas.

After this, mark out on the floor the position where the hearth will be installed. Bear in mind that the wall may well not be straight, so after installation it may be necessary to fill in any small gaps with a coloured resin to match the hearth.

The next stage is to prepare a bedding mixture of sand and cement (or simply tile adhesive) and lay the hearth. Either material can be used but you may find sand and cement easier as it will be easier to adjust the level of the hearth. The best way to ensure the hearth is level is to use a spirit level. Remember to check the level across the fireplace and well as checking the front to back dimension. The back of the hearth will touch the wall when it is in position.

The next step is to install the back panel. In some cases there is a purpose-built void within the marble fire surround to recess a fire; this is usually the case when it is to be fitted against a flat wall. By bringing the back panel away from the wall, a void is created to recess a fire. In this case you would need to fill the void with suitable filler material and bring the back panel away from the wall. If there is a void and you will be installing a gas fire then you will need to fill the void with a suitable non-combustible material.

There may be no void within the fireplace to recess a fire, and this is usually the case if the marble fireplace surround is to be fitted against a chimney. Simply apply some tile adhesive and stick the back panel against the wall. Make sure you spread the adhesive all over the back of the piece of stone and then fix it to the wall. Do not spot dab the adhesive as this will cause a build-up of water through the lining, which can mark the stone.

When the hearth and lining have been installed it is time to fix the legs. You should position the legs carefully, checking that the inside measurement matches the size of the mantle. It is a good idea to mark the position of the legs against the wall. After this, apply some tile adhesive to the fireplace legs and fix them to the wall.

The header and the mantle are positioned last. Simply apply a small amount of clear silicon to the header and mantle to hold it in position. Using a flexible adhesive like clear silicon makes it easier to remove the mantle if needed at a later date.

After you have fixed the fireplace it is important to leave it for several days to dry out. Once you are certain the fireplace is completely dry you should seal it with a normal impregnating stone sealer. You should apply three coats of sealer to

Will My Fire Fit?

A fireplace rebate is the recess depth within a fire surround to recess a fire. If you are installing a fireplace against a flat wall with no recess then you will need to have a fireplace built with a custom void (known as a rebate) to accommodate the depth of your fire, and ensure your fire fits flush.

any limestone hearth (especially if it has a light colour).

Please note that if you are burning wood or coal in the fireplace it is natural for the fire to drop onto the hearth. It is generally a good idea to clean the hearth regularly and thoroughly to ensure any stains are removed and do not build up.

CHAPTER 8

Installing a Patio

The first thing to make sure of with any external installation is that the stone is frost-proof – check this with your retailer. The second major point is to ensure that the base for the patio is laid with a fall so that standing water cannot sit on the stone but drains away.

The other major point is to consider the method of installation. This will normally depend on the base on which you lay the stone. If the base is concrete the installation is more straightforward. The best finish will be obtained by laying the stone with tile adhesive in the manner described for internal stone, which will give you a durable and high-quality floor on a firm, hard base. This method also gives you a wider range of materials to choose from, as a stone of any depth can be laid on a concrete base as long as it is frost-proof.

If the bed is not concrete it will be necessary to install the patio with sand and cement, which is a more time-consuming process. It also means that ideally you should select a material which is at least 2cm thick – preferably 3cm – as well as being frost-proof. The method of installation is not difficult but is different and the key points are outlined below. You may also be dealing with material that has variations in depth.

KEY TOOLS

Thicker stone is obviously heavier and you should be aware of this. It may be good idea to wear a back brace to allow for the extra weight of the larger flagstones.

You will also need the following tools:

- String, stakes and a garden hose

- Spade and shovel
- Pieces of 2in × 4in and 2in × 8in pieces of timber
- Landscape fabric (to stop weeds getting into the patio)
- Mini sledgehammer and rubber mallet
- Tamping tool
- Saw, hammer and nails
- Gloves
- Carpenter's level and tape measure
- Stone sealer.

PREPARATION

The first stage is to pick as level a spot as possible for your patio. If you start on level ground it will be much easier to ensure that the finished patio is level.

Before you start you need to measure the patio area. If the patio is to be 10m × 8m, for example, you should stretch a tape measure to the length of 10m on one side of the proposed patio and mark this length with a string tied between two stakes. Then measure out the 8m width in the same way and again mark both sides with string and stake. Finally, close the string and stake rectangle with a fourth piece of string. Before going further you should check the diag-onal measurements to ensure the space is totally rectangular.

BUILDING THE BASE

The next step is to start work with a spade. Dig down approximately 10cm around the perimeter of the space you have just measured, then, with a digging shovel, dig out all the earth to a depth of

Two different finishes of the same slate in an external situation – as a honed worktop and on the floor in its riven form.

10cm within the perimeter. Use a level to try to dig this area as flat as you possibly can.

The next step is to take a large piece of wood and place it on the ground so that it runs the length of the rectangle on the left-hand side. Put a level on the plank and to check It Is flat. You can adjust the level by scraping away earth to make the appropriate adjustment. Repeat this process on the right-hand side of the rectangle, then across the width of the rectangle. Then you can be confident that you have made the base as level as you can.

The next stage is to moisten the soil with a garden hose and tamp it down with a tamping tool. After this you should lay a landscape fabric down over the base to stop any weeds coming through the patio later on.

The next step is to frame the rectangle. The most effective way to do this is to nail together four 2in × 4in pieces of wood and use them to enclose the 10m × 8m area. This frame will act as a mould and will also contain the layer of sand and stop it spilling out from the area.

Now it is time to apply the sand and spread it in the designated area. Cut another piece of 2in × 4in to a length of 8in × 2in to act as a screed. Starting at one length of the rectangle, slide this screed across the full length of the sand layer. This will help to level the sand and distribute the high points in the sand into the lower areas. This should give you an even surface. If the screed will not slide easily then you need to remove some sand from the rectangle. Afterwards tamp the sand down with a tamping tool.

LAYING THE STONE

Now it is time to lay the stone. Begin in one corner, placing the stone pieces down into the sand and trying to keep the gaps between the stones as

An external riven paving patio being installed. This will always be laid on sand and cement.

small as possible. Use a rubber mallet to gently tap the stones into place. Using your carpenter's level, keep checking that the stones you have laid are level. If any stones have sunk too low you should lift them and place more sand underneath them.

If a piece of stone is too large to fit into a space you should mark it with a pencil to show where the cut should be. Lift the stone and cut it with a tile saw. If you have chosen an antiqued or aged floor you may need to antique the edge of the stone with a chisel so that it replicates the look of the other tiles. This is a simple process that involves making very gentle chips with the chisel up and down the edge of the stone until you are satisfied.

When all of the stone tiles have been laid, pour more sand on top of the patio and then use a broom to sweep it across the patio. The sand will fill up the joints between the tiles.

At this stage you should remove the wooden frame and dispose of it. Fill in the vacant trough with sand and firmly tamp it down using the butt end of a piece of 2in × 4in or an offcut of one of the pieces of stone.

Finally, you need to seal the stone. A normal impregnating sealer is the best thing to use. You should apply three coats of sealer, allowing each coat to dry before applying the next. Take good care to wipe away any residue from the sealer

between each coat. You will find that some external flagstones will absorb vast amounts of sealer. This is normal. It is important to make sure you apply enough sealer, as without this the stone will always have some amount of porosity.

Please note that stone laid in this method, although easier to install than using adhesive and grout, will take more maintenance. It is quite normal for a patio to settle and the only way to rectify this is to lift any sunken tiles, add more sand and level the stone flagstones again.

A tile being sealed. The sealer has been applied with a cloth. The tiles need to be sealed three times during installation.

CHAPTER 9

Care and Maintenance

Once it is sealed correctly, looking after a stone floor, or other stone feature, should be very simple. The basic rules are listed below.

CLEANING

Once the floor has been laid and sealed the care and maintenance required is low. The floor should be mopped with a recommended stone cleaner or water. The best cleaner currently on the market in the UK is Easycare manufactured by Lilothin, although any non-detergent-based cleaner should be suitable. These can be sourced from your stone supplier or any good local DIY store.

It is vitally important never to use any cleaner that contains detergents, as repeated use of detergents can strip the sealer from the floor. A sealer will protect the floor from most stains, but care must still be taken with oil- and acid-based products. Spillages should be cleaned as soon as detected. Any stain that does occur can be cleaned with an intensive stone cleaner. Marks on limestone floors are very rare.

If you do inadvertently use detergent on your floor it need not necessarily be a cause for concern. You should test the effectiveness of the sealer if you have any doubt in your mind, by simply splashing small amounts of water on the floor in four or five different places. If, after about forty-five or sixty seconds, it wipes away with a paper towel without leaving a water mark, then your sealer is working properly. If it does leave a water mark this indicates that there is an issue with the performance of the sealer. The most common solution for this would be to reseal the floor.

How often you clean is down to personal choice. Some clients clean their floor every one or two days while other home owners choose to clean the floor much less frequently. The important point is to use the correct cleaners and to treat the floor as any other floor in terms of day-to-day maintenance.

A typical floor cleaner. There are many different brands you can use, but it is important to remember never to use detergent on a stone floor.

RESEALING

After a period of time you will need to reseal your floor. This will involve applying an intensive cleaner (such as Wexa) to the floor to remove all the sealer. After this, the floor should be washed with water to remove any dust or dirt. When the floor is dry the floor should be sealed in the same way it was done originally (described in Chapter 5). It is important to follow the advice of the stone supplier with regard to when this should be done. It is normal to expect to reseal a high-density floor every four to five years. Remember you can always check how effective the sealer on the floor is by testing with a glass of water as described above.

ACID MARKING

Any limestone or marble is slightly alkaline in nature so can be vulnerable to damage from acidic liquids such as fruit juice, red wine or things of similar nature. If you drop anything acidic on a natural stone floor wipe it up as soon as you can. If you leave it on the floor for any length of time there is a small chance it could mark the floor. This is not caused by a failure of the sealer but is simply the result of the acid eating into the surface of the stone. If this happens you will notice a small mark on the floor, and if you touch it you will feel the surface of the stone is slightly etched. It is now possible to buy a specialist cleaning product that will remove the mark. This cleaner will also repair the sheen of the stone so that the etching cannot be seen. If this happens to your floor, try in the first instance to contact the person who sold you the stone and seek their advice on the best way forward.

WAXING

It is possible to improve the look of some natural stones by using waxes or alternative care products. Traditionally, wax was always used on stone floors to protect the stone before the advent of sealers, so waxing the floor is a good way to replicate a traditional flagstone look. This is normally carried out after sealing and can be done with a buffing machine or by hand. The important points

are to ensure you get equal coverage of wax across the floor and that any residue is removed. If possible, use a buffing machine as this will make it much easier to get equal coverage; buff until there is a sheen across the floor.

Any floor will need to be rewaxed periodically. It is difficult to specify when this should be done as it depends on the amount of wear on the floor. It is normally possible to see when this needs to be done because the sheen wears the floor and it starts to look duller,.

The process of rewaxing the floor is simple. First, clean it carefully with a cleaning product – widely available from any stone retailer – to remove the wax. Then wash the floor with water and finally, apply the new wax with the buffing machine.

CARE PRODUCTS

There is a variety of other care products that can be used on flooring. If you have an open-grained natural stone you may need to put a care product on the surface to stop dirt getting ground into the surface. The best product on the market in the UK is called Multiseal. This forms a protective layer on the top of the stone and is applied after the sealer, as it is a surface treatment. The process will need to be repeated every year but can be done without professional input. The process involves cleaning the floor by hand and making a big effort to remove any loose dirt; hiring a buffing machine will speed up this process. Once the floor is clean you can apply the Multiseal then buff the floor to ensure equal coverage to all areas. It is important to ensure that any residue is removed from the floor.

FILLING HOLES IN TRAVERTINE

As discussed earlier a feature of a travertine floor which has been filled is that over time small holes will develop in the floor. This is natural and a feature of travertine. To rectify this you do not need to bring in a tiler, but instead source a hard, white epoxy resin. This can be applied to the floor with a trowel and should be skimmed to ensure the filler is level with the surface of the floor. Then just leave it to set.

EXTERNAL STONE

External stone requires the same care and main-tenance as internal stone, and needs to be re-sealed and cleaned with the same products. Again, it is important not to use detergent-based cleaners. You can use a pressure washer to clean an external stone terrace or patio. If your external terrace has an area where sunlight is limited it is possible that algae or moss will grow on the stone. This is easy to remove. The best approach is to contact the stone retailer to source a specialist cleaner for algae. This is normally applied with a brush and simple to use.

Conclusion

How to install a stone floor, as well as other stone features such as kitchen worktops and a fireplace have been covered.

By the time you have reached this section you should be looking back at the results of a fairly exhausting but rewarding process. Installing any stone product needs to be done methodically and steadily, but once complete the job will give you a floor, fireplace, worktop or similar that is hardwearing, durable and will last for many years. It will also bring the natural beauty of stone into your home.

The maintenance of natural stone is also straightforward as long as it is tackled systematically, and is usually simply a matter of using the correct cleaning programme as advised by the retailer. From my experience the vast majority of people who have problems with stone floors suffer them because they do not carry out the installation correctly or do not maintain the floor properly. The lesson is clear – follow the instructions and enjoy the beauty of the natural stone in your home for years to come.

In this kitchen the black granite has been selected to match the black Aga. The cream kitchen cupboards provide an effective complement to the stone top.

This contemporary Portuguese limestone floor, called St Luke, has been laid with an oak kitchen. This floor gives a clean, modern appearance. Martin Moore and Co.

These large flagstones have been laid across this space rather than lengthways to make the space look larger. Martin Moore and Co.

Glossary

Acid-washed   Stone washed with acid to accelerate the antiquing process.

Brick bond   A common pattern of installing rectangular tiles in a staggered or offset fashion, creating the look of a brick wall.

Brushed finish   A method of ageing the surface of a stone by brushing it with a coarse wire rotary brush. This causes the surface to take on a worn, leathery appearance.

Border   A decorative piece of stone that is normally long and narrow and is set within the floor to create interest.

Bullnose   Rounding an exposed stone edge.

Bush-hammered   A mechanical method of beating the surface of a stone tile to give it an aged finish.

Cabochon   Small, square tiles that are traditionally inserted into the space where four larger square tiles meet. This is a traditional method of laying stone in a hallway. They are normally darker stones inserted into a light-coloured floor.

Calibrated   When a stone tile has been cut with a saw on both sides to create a consistent thickness.

Chamfered edge   A bevelled tile edge.

Chequerboard   The name for a floor pattern with alternate square tiles of differing stones. This is commonly laid in hallways.

Chiselled edge   A process of chipping the tile edge either by hand or by machine to create a rustic edge.

Cladding   Slabs of stone used to face a wall.

Cleft finish   A stone that has a rough surface, normally created by the way the material is split in the quarry along its natural plane. It is commonly associated with slate or sandstone from India.

Cobblestone   A stone that appears to be naturally round due to many years of wear.

Cross-cut   Stone that has been cut across the block rather than parallel to the natural bedding plane. This tends to give a mottled, cloud-like appearance and is normally found in travertine.

Efflorescence   This is the appearance of white, powder-like substances on the surface of the stone or grout. This is normally an accumulation of salt caused by a build-up of moisture.

Face   The portion of a tile or slab that is exposed.

Filled stone   This is another term primarily associated with travertine. It normally refers to open pores or fossil holes being filled with epoxy resin or grout.

Flagstone   Usually large, thick pieces of stone in varying sizes used in traditional properties.

Flame texture   A textured, rough surface usually created through direct application of intense heat. It is normally associated with granite or limestone.

Gang saw   This is a large, water-driven saw that cuts raw blocks of stone into pieces of specified thickness.

Gauged stone   Stone tiles ground by machine to ensure uniform depth.

Granite   A hard, crystalline, igneous rock formation formed from extreme heat, comprised of minerals such as quartz and feldspar.

Grout   A cement-based or epoxy material used to fill in joints between tiles. This is available in a wide range of colours.

Herringbone   A traditional rustic method of setting rectangular tiles in a slanted pattern, creating a zigzag effect.

Honed finish   A sharp, satin-smooth finish to the face of a stone tile. This is generally the first process applied to a stone tile when cut.

Igneous   A type of rock formed by the cooling and solidification of molten matter over thousands of years.

Inserts   Small, square tiles inserted into the space where four larger square tiles meet. This is a traditional method of laying stone in a hallway. Usually the inserts are darker stones set into a light-coloured floor.

Joint   The area where two tiles or two slabs meet.

Limestone   A rock formed from the sedimentary process, generally underground and underwater, which is primarily made up of calcium deposits such as fossil and shell.

Marble   A limestone that has a heavy concentration of quartz, which is generally polished to give a high-sheen finish.

Metamorphic rock   A type of rock that has been altered in appearance by intense pressure and/or heat.

Mosaic   Small pieces of coloured stone that are mounted onto a mesh and are often laid out to create a pattern or a design.

Onyx   A translucent, banded type of marble that is generally found in caves.

Pallet   A strong wooden frame on which stone tiles are normally shipped from the quarry.

Parquetry   An inlaid floor made up of geometric shapes and two or more stone types and/or colours.

Patina   The surface of a stone when it has changed in texture and/or colour due to age and wear.

Pillowed   A hand finish applied to give a soft, rounded finish to the edges of a tile.

Polished finish   A high-gloss, shiny finish that can be achieved on very hard stones. Polished finishes work best on stones with deep colours and tones, where they draw out the full colour of the stone.

Quarry   Where the blocks of stone are removed from the ground.

Quartzite   A stone mainly composed of sandstone and the mineral quartz.

Sandblasted   A textured, rough surface that is achieved by blasting sand at high pressure onto the face of the stone.

Sandstone   A sedimentary rock consisting primarily of quartz that is held together by silica or calcium carbonate.

Saw cut A rough, textured finish in which you can see the circular saw marks created when the stone was cut from the block. This finish is very slip resistant and gives a rustic appearance. It is only suitable for external use.

Slab A linear piece of stone cut from the block. It is generally used for the manufacture of counter tops or large pieces of stone.

Slate A natural stone generally composed of shale and clay.

Splashback In a bathroom, the area between the vanity top and the cabinet. This is normally 20–40cm high. In a kitchen, the part of the wall behind the hob.

Split face A finish with a rough, riven face where the stone has been split from another piece of stone (rather than sawn) in the quarry.

Travertine A natural stone that is similar to limestone. It is normally formed near hot bubbling springs, which create its naturally pitted surface. It has to be filled either with resin or grout.

Tumbled finish An aged finish created by placing the stone in a drum or tumbling machine. This process softens the edge of the stone and creates a worn, traditional effect.

Unfilled A stone that has pits and holes on its surface that have not been filled with epoxy resin at the quarry.

Vein cut Stone that has been cut from the block perpendicular to the natural plane. This technique tends to exaggerate and enhance any natural veins in the stone and is normally used on travertine or marble.

Weathering Antiquing the surface of a stone.

Index